My Walk With Christ ✝

When You Pray, Believe

Pastor Neruka White &

Minister Judy Creighton

Published by

Peaches
Publications

Published in London by Peaches Publications, 2024.

www.peachespublications.co.uk

The moral right of the author has been asserted.

All rights reserved. No part of this book may be reproduced, stored in a retrieval system, or transmitted in any form or by any means, electronic, mechanical, photocopying, recording, public performances or otherwise, without written permission of Neruka White and Judy Creighton, except for brief quotations embodied in critical articles or reviews. The workbook is for personal use only; commercial use is prohibited unless written permission and a license is obtained from the author Neruka White & Judy Creighton.

Book Cover Image courtesy of Pixbay.

The right of Neruka White and Judy Creighton to be identified as the author of this work has been asserted in accordance with sections 77 and 78 of the copyright Designs and Patents Act 1988.

Text Copyright © 2024 by Neruka White and Judy Creighton

British Library Cataloguing in Publication Data: A catalogue record for this book is available from the British Library.

Unless otherwise stated, scripture quotations are taken from the Holy Bible, The Authorised King James Version (KJV). Scripture marked MSG, is taken from The Message. Copyright 1993,1994, 1995, 1996, 2000, 2002. Used by permission of NavPress Publishing Group. Scripture marked AMP is taken from the Amplified. Copyright 1954,1958,1962,1965, 1987 by the Lockman Foundation.

ISBN: 9798328528900

Book cover design: Peaches Publications LTD.

Editor: Shelley Sanger.

Typesetter: Winsome Duncan.

Proofreader: Shelley Sanger.

Table of Contents

DEDICATION 1

ACKNOWLEDGEMENTS 2

PREFACE 4

FOREWORD 8

ENDORSEMENTS 11

GOD IS LISTENING 15

PASTOR NERUKA WHITE 16

    IN THE BEGINNING… 16

A JOURNEY OF ENLIGHTENMENT 35

    FINDING MY VOICE 48
    A WONDROUS REVELATION 52
    BEAUTIFULLY BROKEN 58
    YOU CAN'T KILL PURPOSE 63

WHEN YOU PRAY BELIEVE 67

    MINISTER JUDY CREIGHTON 67
    PRAY ALWAYS 83
    BEAUTY IN HUMILITY 84
    COUNT THE COST 89
    POTENT LOVE 94
    THE POWER OF GOD'S LOVE 95
    BELIEVE VERSUS UNBELIEF 95
    GOD SUPPLIED NEEDS 98

MOTIVATING SCRIPTURES 101

INSPIRING POETRY CORNER 109

    BEAUTY IN POWER 117
    BEING ME, BEING YOU 118

    WHAT IS FAITH 119
    SOMETIMES I FEEL LIKE A FRAUD 120
    CELEBRATE 121
    PURPOSE CANNOT DIE 123
    CHOOSING CHRIST IS THE ONLY CHOICE 125
    THE ECHOES OF STRENGTH 130
    BELIEVE IT IS DONE 131

MINISTER JUDY'S POEMS 135
    GOD WATCH OVER YOU 136
    LOVE WORTH FINDING 138
    GOD SEES YOU 139
    CRAZY LOVE 140
    CHURCH LIFE 141
    THE FIVE SENSES OF LOVE 142
    TAKE COURAGE AND TRY 143
    FIGHT 144
    MY HEART YIELDS 145
    LET ME SING 146
    BRAND NEW START 147
    VICTORY IN JESUS NAME 148

INSPIRING QUOTES 149

LETTER TO MY YOUNGER SELF 167

FAVOURITE GOSPEL SONGS 172

EPILOGUE 175
    THE IMPORTANCE OF PRAYER 175

ABOUT THE AUTHORS 179

REFLECTIONS STUDY NOTES 185

My Walk with Christ

Dedication

This is dedicated to the memory of my beloved paternal grandma, Ms Adeline Harding who I fondly describe as my guardian angel, from the day I was born until she became too ill to leave her home.

Pastor Neruka White

To my son Donald Buddington and my four grandchildren: Alberto, Dominic, Joseph and Gracie. To my sister Precious and my three brothers.

Minister Judy Creighton

Acknowledgements

First and foremost, my heart is filled with gratitude to my Father Jesus Christ, who blessed me with a life filled with testimonies of His love and faithfulness. I am extremely grateful to my family who have always supported me in all my ventures, no matter how wild or extraordinary.

In loving memory to my grandma Adeline Harding, my human guardian angel; and my children who always encouraged me to keep writing.

Thank you to my various pastors who have taught, corrected and guided me to the truth of *walking with Christ* and to? Minister Judy Creighton who was courageous enough to agree to co – author this book with me.

I would also like to give thanks to all the saints who attend the Leeds fasting service, where we explore the different stages of life.

To all my dear friends and brethren, who have prayed for me, corrected me, taught me and refused to let me give up. You know yourselves. I love you all and pray, God will supply your every need.

To Bishop and Mother Richards, our beloved spiritual mom and dad, whose prayers and wise counsel keep us grounded in our faith.

Lastly but by no means least, to Ms Winsome Duncan, for believing in us! Thank you for investing your time, enthusiasm and your skills as a book coach. We must succeed with you guiding us!

Pastor Neruka White

I thank God. He gave me the desire and confidence to pursue my dreams, and fulfil my goal to write and become an author. *"Delight thyself also in the Lord; and He shall give thee the desires of thine heart."*

(PSALMS 37:4 KJV)

I would also like to thank Pastor White, she prophesied by the Holy Ghost that we should write a book. When I heard her prophesy, it resurrected my childhood dream to become an author.

I also would like to thank Winsome Duncan, my publicist and book writing coach, for providing me with the tools to develop my writing skills and make this book become a reality.

Thanks also to the CJCA church family who prayed and encouraged me to 'just do it'.

Minister Judy Creighton

Preface

My walk with Christ started on the day I was born. My grandma told me that on this day, she took me outside in the yard, lifted me up towards Heaven and said a prayer of dedication of my life to the Lord.

Today I am grateful for:

The breath of life.

A better understanding of what can happen if I take my focus away from God's direction and purpose for my life.

The chance to repent of my decisions to go my own way and to put my own interpretation on what is happening in and to me.

Today I say to the Lord: I am sorry for trying to organise my life by my own understanding. Please Lord Jesus help me to be obedient to you. To learn from your life decisions when you walked this earth as a man.

You journeyed in stages and showed perfection in the way that you lived out your purpose, stage by stage. You never allowed anyone or any circumstances to change or interfere with the process of your journey; you lived as a man, being God in flesh, come to redeem fallen humanity.

With love and compassion you stooped down and made clay to open my eyes, because I was born blind.

"You spoke deliverance into my Spirit, when I was brought down so low. You said Woman, thou art loosed"!

My body was broken, there was nothing left to spend, no hope to get well they said,: but I pushed through to touch you. My Soul longed to hear: by faith you have touched me and now you are healed

You gave your life, faced death and won the victory for my sake, to bring me back to life. You taught me to live in and by your Word, to know who I am and why I am here. By faith I am now part of your plan of continued salvation for the world. You saved me and commissioned me to be a WITNESS.

Lord please cleanse my heart and make my steps strong. Give me good understanding and wisdom to make right choices. Remove from me confusion and make me see clearly. May I live with courage and make right decisions. Cover me Lord and keep me from all evil.

"May 'your good acceptable and perfect will' be my heart's desire in every decision I make."

(Romans 12:3)

Lord, I accept the commission you have given me. I believe that I was born for this purpose. May I learn to serve in your Body and to the world with integrity, with compassion, with honesty and truth. Amen.
"How can two walk together except they be agreed?" Yet we follow Jesus and say: Where He may lead me, I will go for I have learned to trust Him so.

It is easier to follow or walk with a friend or an acquaintance. Without trust it is unlikely that anyone would be willing to follow a stranger.

Therefore, when we walk with Jesus it requires faith and trust. For we walk by faith and not by sight."

(2 Cor 5:7 KJV)

"Life's path way is rough sometimes. The road that we travel could be fraught with trouble. Man that is born of a woman is of few days, and full of trouble."
(Job 14:1 KJV)

"The obstacles you encounter may slow you down. Though the pace seems slow, keep on walking. Your set back could be your come back. Never give up until you have reached your goal.

Every obstacle is a learning experience that can help build our character and strengthen our faith in Jesus Christ.

Jesus leads and guides us. He protects us from dangers. He promises that He will never leave us, nor forsake us. He promises to supply all our needs. We have just got to trust Him. Walking with Him could be an adventure.

Nobody said it would be easy, sometimes it seems like the whole world is against you. Have you ever seen a storm? The wind and the rain is threatening, but do not be afraid, Jesus is with you. He will rise up and He will say, Peace be still."

(Mark 4:29 KJV)

"Whatever your experiences are in life, you could say, as Job did: "I would seek unto God, and unto God would I commit my cause. Which doeth great things and unsearchable; marvellous things without number."
(Job 5:8-9 KJV)

FOREWORD

As the National Bishop of Church of Jesus Christ Apostolic UK, I have had the opportunity of delivering sermons to different congregations. The zeal to have an in-depth knowledge of the scriptures led me to pursue a Bachelor of Theology and Doctor of Divinity. In order to further fulfil the needs of my immediate and the wider congregation, I also pursued and obtained a diploma in Psychological Counselling. It is through the leading of the Holy Spirit and the revelations from the Lord, that I am able to deliver the Word of God with humility and servitude.

I deem it an honour to be asked by authors Pastor Neruka White and Minister Judy Creighton to write the foreword for this book. I have personally known Pastor Neruka White for a good number of years but it wasn't until after the passing of the bishop of her assembly, that I got to realise her true leadership skills, determination and drive. She has ministered in different capacities in the church community, in the offices of Evangelist, Sunday school teacher and currently as Senior Pastor in her Assembly. I have been blessed to listen to her sharing the Word of God on numerous forums and platforms. She has always left an indelible mark on her readers and listeners by using her life experiences to further expound on the goodness and mercies of God, His compassion and love towards her.

Minister Judy Creighton is a dynamic and powerful woman of God who I had the pleasure of meeting when she visited the Church of Jesus Christ Apostolic in Darnall a few years ago. I was moved by her charismatic way of delivering the Word of God and her ability to connect with her audience. Minister Creighton is anointed to teach and minister the Word of God with much authority.

The authors have a passion for studying the Word of God and seeking to increase in the wisdom and knowledge of God. This common love and desire for the Word of God helped to fuse these two authors together. They both have a deep desire to enhance the Kingdom of God through the winning of souls. As a result, Pastor White has reached out to the lost through community and other, overseas projects.

Pastor Neruka White has been writing spiritual podcasts and a series of devotionals for quite some time. It was therefore no surprise when she mentioned that she was writing a book to be co-authored by Minister Judy Creighton. In their book, 'My Walk with Christ', the authors have shown their constant faith when faced with adversities and their complete dependence on God. Readers will appreciate the genuine honesty being revealed on each page. If you are looking for a

Christian life that is trouble-free then you will not find that in this book. What 'My Walk With Christ' does, is show that God is in control and Philippians 1 verse 6 demonstrates being confident of this very thing, that "He who begun a good work in you will complete it until the day of Jesus Christ." Pastor White and Minister Creighton truly believe this and therefore have based their whole lives on being rooted and firmly grounded in Christ, which the book clearly depicts. This book will not only capture the spiritual minds of its readers but will also help those who are at a crossroads in their lives where it seems as if there is no hope. As you embark on the journey with the authors and their walk with Christ throughout this book, may your lives be transformed and may you have an encounter with the Lord and Saviour Jesus Christ that will help you in your walk with Him.

As an evangelist and a minister, I have no doubt that it is the desire of the authors to win souls for Christ through their book. For a soul to surrender and give their life to Jesus Christ through the reading of 'My Walk With Christ' would mean that the book has fulfilled its purpose. May God bless Pastor White and Minister Creighton as they continue to work for the Master.

Bishop Dr. Cebert T Richards (DD)

National Bishop, Church of Jesus Christ Apostolic UK

ENDORSEMENTS

"Train up a child in the way he should go, And even when he is old, he will not depart from it."

(Proverbs 22:6).

This book takes you down memory lane of the authors' lives. It locks you into their lives growing up as Christians in Jamaica, and their experiences in England. This book speaks about the importance of having God-fearing family members in our lives, the roles they play, and how as children we sometimes take them for granted. I recommend this book, each home should hold a copy. It's a life tool and lesson for all family members.

Missionary Sandra Johnson

Bethel United Church Of Jesus Christ (Apostolic)

First of all, well done to both of you for trusting in Jesus to take the project to this stage. Secondly, your experiences of coming to Christ are so different: one being enveloped in light, and the other through a question after a confession. It is written in the scriptures that: "For with the heart man believeth unto righteousness; and with the mouth confession is made unto salvation.(Romans 10:10 KJV)

Excellent encouraging and uplifting testimonies and God bless you as I wait to see the finished book.

Brother Percy Watt

Pastor Neruka White and Minister Creighton have taken us on a journey of how they found the Lord. Theirs was not an easy one, Both weave through different stages of their lives, describing the joys mixed with sadness and trials mixed with happiness until ultimately, God delivered them. They are who they are today because 'God kept them' and fashioned them through many stages of life to make them the Ambassadors of Christ that we see today. Read and enjoy the Testimonies of God's servants.

Overseer BA Haughton

Church of Jesus Christ Apostolic UK

Dearest Pastor "Ner"

Thank you for the opportunity for allowing me to read and share my thoughts on your latest book 'My Walk With Christ'. It is beautifully written and I loved how you took the time to describe your Grandmother and her mannerisms in such detail.

It reminded me fondly of my own Grandmother.

My Walk with Christ

I was intrigued by the beauty and the heartfelt stories of your childhood memories and ultimately your acceptance of and the coming to our Lord and Saviour Jesus Christ.

I was also particularly tickled by the use of Patois throughout the narrative and how you translated certain sentences into English. Although my Patois is a little rusty, I could hear the sweetness of the Jamaican accent when reading what you wrote.

A truly beautiful sentiment.

Good use of encouraging bible scriptures which are well spaced out. Good use of dialogue within the text.

I cannot wait to read a signed copy of your completed book. It feels like I know you just a little bit more today than I did at the beginning of the week.

Your son in Christ.

Dr Audley Fraser
Dip MT Hons, Lic TMS, OSTm MAO
Dr of Osteomyology

Two incredible stories of the authors' faith walk with Jesus. Inspiring, funny, moving and encouraging. 'When we walk with the Lord, in the light of His word, what a glory He sheds on our way,' are the words of an old songwriter. Neruka and Judy truly show the rewards of trusting, being obedient to God, even in adversity, and being determined to succeed. A good honest read, medicine for the soul and encouragement for life's journey.

Hazel Barrett

This book is inspiring. The beautiful relationship between the author and her grandmother is heart-warming. The experiences of how prayer and faith changed the author's life is encouraging. If you want to know how faith in God can make a difference in your life, read this book

Angela Tulloch
Evangelist

GOD IS LISTENING

Pastor Neruka White

In the beginning…

As I reflect back to the very beginning of my life's journey I recall my beloved Granny, Adeline Harding, inimitable matriarch of our branch of the Harding family; mother of four sons, one daughter, two grandchildren and growing, once more recounting the tale of what happened on the day I was born. Although she had told it many times before, today it felt like the first time. So I sat quietly next to her chair, rested my head on her lap with my eyes slightly closed, as her voice compelled me to travel back in time and imagine this unforgettable day.

Granny was wearing her usual bright floral skirt that gathered at her seemingly small waist, flowing over her beautifully rounded hips almost to her ankles. The fabric felt comfy and soothing on my face so I scrunched up a little of the hem in my right hand and stuck my left thumb in my mouth. I gazed at up at her dark chocolate brown face that glowed with perspiration on her nose and cheeks. She had just had a hot flush and was swishing the hem of her skirt to try and direct cool air to her face. My nostrils filled with citrus and minty fragrances from her clothes and hands. Her hair was plaited in the same style as always; soft grey hair with dark strands weaving through to the end of each plait, hugging her cheeks. Granny took a deep breath and drew her chair closer to the window.

We rented and lived in this spacious room which was part of a large house. There was a double bed placed near the window to catch the morning sun, a dining table with four chairs in the middle and various storage cabinets along the walls. Bright floral curtains hung at the windows, which were always slightly open, and fluttered in the breeze, balancing the otherwise stifling heat.

Granny might have been there when I was born from the emotional and vivid way she described what happened, yet I'll never really know for sure.

Wednesday 20th June 1962, a day like no other, I entered the world a tiny bundle of joy. Like all my mother's children, I was born at home; for me, this was a little house on Old Harbour Road in Spanish Town, St Catherine, Jamaica.

On this particular day it was scorching hot, typical of the Caribbean just at the start of the hurricane season. The heat and humidity rose in bright shimmering waves of colour bringing to mind the image of a Phoenix rising from the ashes. In spite of the heat, a strong gusty wind shook the branches of the trees, spreading some well needed cool air along the path, warning of the coming rain, which could suddenly gush down in a heavy downpour and disappear as suddenly as it came.

Granny gently lifted me from my mum's tired arms and carried me outside into the yard, where she carefully raised me up towards Heaven and offered a prayer of dedication over me to welcome her first granddaughter into the world and commit me to the safety of our Father God.

This story made such a great impact on me that when my own children and grandchildren were born, I carried on the tradition of dedicating each of them to the service of the Lord as soon after their birth as I could. I made sure to ask for God's blessings and protection over their precious lives, following in the footsteps of the matriarch of our family, a lady of honour, honesty and compassion; dedicated to following Christ and leading her family members to an awareness of God's majesty and awesome power and at the same time rejoicing in His lowliness and loving kindness for all His creation (Matthew 11:29).

I believe that by praying for me on the day I was born, Granny became my very own guardian angel. I spent most of my childhood living with her and I believe with all my heart that God used her to save my life on many occasions. I don't think I would have made it to adulthood without the constant presence of my Granny and the strong bond we had.

The first time Granny came to my rescue I was about fourteen months old and still not yet walking on my own. It broke her heart to see me struggling to keep my balance; I wasn't managing at all well. She told me that I could move pretty fast on my bottom as I chased my toys across the floor, and how I laughed and clapped my hands as I tried to catch a soft toy my mum tossed up in the air. My mum, who was still in her late teens and probably expecting my sister at the time, was in obvious need of help, especially with my dad away at work all day. Granny had a brilliant idea! Somehow she convinced my mum to let her take care of me for a while and try out an ancient home remedy passed down from her grandparents.

Granny shared countless stories about ancient natural herbal remedies. Some of which were used to ease us, her children and grandchildren, through the growing pains of the common cold, mumps, chickenpox, cuts and bruises. These rather obscure but possibly lifesaving remedies would also have been used by Granny's mother Susan Myrie, whom she spoke about at every opportunity; which is probably why I still remember her name. Granny sounded so confident in her belief that it would work, that she didn't let on to my mum how adventurous my stay with her would be. Granny knew exactly what to do.

The ancient remedy was a blue powder, known as Indigo. This multipurpose mineral was mainly used in the old days to brighten white clothing when added to the water in which they were rinsed. Who would have guessed that it had healing properties?

My Walk with Christ

For nine consecutive days, a bath half filled with water was left outside overnight so dew would fall into it. Very early each morning, before the sun came up, Granny would bathe me in the water for a few minutes. I screamed at the discomfort when the icy water touched my tiny body but Granny always sang softly to soothe me as she gently patted it onto my hips, "Hush mama baby mama gone a market papa gone a grung (field). Aunty gone fi wata, sista mek up di fiah, (fire)bredda peel di food." Then she did with me what her mum and my mum encouraged us to do with our own children as young mothers, she stretched my limbs. It would have possibly looked like torture but was actually very strengthening, and done with the greatest care in a safe place to prevent accidents.

After the nine early mornings of Indigo bath and stretch, Granny continued to take me out early every morning for walks, hitched on her hip, "to get fresh air," she said. She prayed for me every day, believing that love would make me strong. Gradually, she noticed my little legs getting steadier as I grasped the table, chair or a grown up's leg to pull myself up. Grasping tightly at Granny's, I looked up at her with big bright eyes and she said, "Come Nehneh, come mi Pinckney walk fi Granny." Then one day I stood up on my own. Granny shouted to everyone nearby, " Come and see, come and look at Ner, walking! Praise God." Day by day the miracle became more apparent. Oh the joy Granny felt when she finally saw her precious grandchild not only walking, but running and dancing! Granny burst forth in grateful song with one of her favourite choruses, "Oh happy Day!"

God answered Granny's prayers and rewarded her faith. I believe she was inspired by the Lord. He blessed her efforts and filled her heart with compassion for a baby girl who needed her at such a crucial time. From that time onwards the bond that was created on the day of my birth continued to grow stronger and stronger.

My Granny and I had an especially close relationship that lasted throughout my childhood and many life challenging situations, most of which I spent living with her. Granny played the role of mother, father and guardian angel. She seemed to have a strong spiritual connection with me that no matter where I was, if I was in serious danger she would come and get me, even from my parents' homes. She would just say, "Me come fe Ner". Everyone called me Ner. She would get me dressed and off we would go, to safety. She never explained how she knew that I needed her. I She might have sensed that I was left at home alone too often, or not eating properly.

When I was five my mum took me home to live with her in Kingston, the capital of Jamaica. We lived across the street from the cinema. Saturday morning matinees were often enjoyed by mum and me when she wasn't at work. The house was on the main street in Three Miles. Possibly so named because it was about three miles from downtown

Kingston. Mum worked in a restaurant almost next-door to the cinema. It was a very long street filled with a variety of interesting looking clothing and furniture shops, garages, schools and an empty bit of land where children would gather to play after school. The street stretched all the way to downtown, popularly known as Parade; it was the main shopping area and included the very famous Coronation Market.

Mum sent me to a wonderful prep school, that I loved attending. I remember my time there so clearly because my teacher, who seemed to have spent some time in Europe, taught us the metric tables. I recall all the children's enthusiastic singsong voices reciting: ten millimetres, one centimetre, ten centimetres, one decimetre, ten decimates, one metre. At five years old we were way ahead of most children because Jamaica was using the old system, until the mid-seventies.

I was a fussy eater. Most parents will have experienced at least one child who just didn't appreciate good food, I was that one. Skinny as a bean pole, and in Granny's words, snaky, bony and scarce of fat. My mum, was also small in body, yet strong and big boned. She was dark skinned with bright dark eyes and beautiful black hair, which she always kept under a scarf. She was full of what felt like electric energy. Whenever she entered a space everyone noticed her without her speaking a word.

She was a wonderful cook but I didn't like her food. She made cornmeal porridge for me but I didn't like cornmeal, so when she wasn't looking I poured it in the bin. I didn't dare tell her that I preferred rice or oat porridge. She noticed of course, that I wasn't putting on any weight, and being a mum, she tried to encourage me with other foods that were nourishing, like Saturday Soup. Hers was not runny and light like Granny's; it was lovely and thick with ground foods like yams. Yikes! Not for me! At five years old this was like a nightmare. I only liked rice and dumplings. No vegetables, thank you! Mum caught me pouring her rich nourishing soup in the bin one Saturday afternoon and she gave me a sound spanking. Being stubborn and headstrong, I found other ways to get rid of the foods that I didn't like. I became very unhappy and longed for the familiar comfort and relaxing atmosphere of living with my Granny. I didn't understand why I couldn't eat the lovely food or why I didn't feel emotionally connected with my mum. When I was with her I missed my Granny, but when I was with Granny, I missed my mum.

One day, Granny turned up. What a surprise! I was overjoyed to see her. My mum wouldn't have been very pleased but when Granny said, "Me come feh Ner," she allowed me to go. She had every intention of getting me back; after all I was her child. Somehow Granny knew that everything was not alright and she needed to come and get me. Off we went, back to Spanish Town.

My Walk with Christ

I didn't realise until much later that I missed certain things about living with my mum: the lovely big airy space indoors, a backyard to play in, a great school and of course my mum. Although I never felt relaxed and comfortable with her, the way I did with Granny. I know she loved me and I loved her too, but we just didn't have a close relationship.

I lived with mum for short periods up until I was fourteen. I decided then that I would stay with Granny because it felt like mum was always disappointed in me. I loved books and school but unlike mum, I wasn't physically strong or particularly active. Maybe I was too much like my dad. My mum wanted me to be more like her, businesslike, even to be less interested in school! I made up my mind to go back and stay with my Granny after living with mum for ten months. I went to see mum occasionally. I still loved her. I learned a lot of skills from her and treasure her memory.

Everything was different here with my Granny. I only remember feeling safe and protected when I saw her. It was like no one and no thing would dare to cause me harm when she was near.

I thrived in Granny's care; as a toddler she taught me to pray, "Our Father who art in Heaven..." morning and night and to recite scriptures like Psalms 1, 23, 100. The words of these Psalms became light in my Soul; they answered unspoken questions at times when I missed my mum and dad or wondered about my siblings. I loved my Granny and there was no doubt that she loved me and treasured me as a special gift from God. Naturally my heart still longed to be with my parents but they had separated when my sister Angela and I were very young.

Both Angela and I lived with Granny for a couple of years; we had a close bond but my precious sister had a disability which meant that she needed a great deal of care and constant attention. Granny struggled to cope with both of us and reluctantly asked my mum to come and get her. Mum had to go to work and Angela was unable to attend school at age four so our mum's mother, Vida Williams who lived over a hundred miles away in Porters Mountain, between Westmorland and Hanover, happily took her and lovingly brought her up. In the country there were more family members to help Grandma Vida, more open spaces, trees, fresh food and fresh air.

Angela thrived there and her health greatly improved. For many years my mum visited them as often as she could, but she was in another relationship and had other children to raise. My sister Angela sadly passed away when she was only twenty-seven years old, from complications with her health condition. I'm so grateful for the precious times we had together and thankful that she got to share in the love and care of both our grandmothers. This gives me immense comfort, especially when I remember how happy she was on the days she was well enough to run about and play with me in the yard, yelling at the top of our voices and chasing each other around the house. We chased butterflies and lizards until we were tired and thirsty. Granny always had a jug of lemonade with ice ready for us. Angela would go to sleep for a while and Granny would sing some of her favourite choruses while she washed our clothes or prepared meals.

Singing was one of Granny's favourite ways to pass the time, a song for every experience and a proverb for every lesson; that was Granny's way. She believed in worshiping the Lord at all times whether we were happy or sad, whether things were going well or not. A thankful heart is a blessing in the sight of God.

"Make a joyful noise unto the Lord all ye lands." (Psalm 100:1a.)

"Aee, beee, ceee, deee," Granny and me learning my ABCs. She taught me how to spell simple words even before most children started Basic school at three years old, which is the Jamaican version of nursery school. I'm not sure whether it was her or my dad who bought be an 'ABC' book, known as a primer. Every child had one back then for when they went to Basic school, so they could practice at home. At two years old I was so ready for Basic school. My cognitive ability to recognise and connect letter sounds were beyond my age. A basic school in Jamaica is usually kept in a church building and children from the age of three are accepted and taught basic skills in the three R's: Reading, wRiting and aRithmetic. At six years old they would be ready to start primary school.

The foundation for my love of books and reading was laid by my Granny. She spent time daily showing me the beauty and excitement of being able to recognise and connect the shapes and sounds of the letters of the alphabet, to reading the words in books. I loved the sounds of different words and memorised their shapes; this served me well in secondary school when I decided that I wanted to learn to spell. I bought a spelling book and spent hundreds of hours memorising the sounds and shapes of all kinds of words. I aced all my spelling tests and soon my classmates were asking me for help with their spelling.

Granny singing her favourite hymns and choruses kept all the grandchildren, as well as the neighbours', who spent time with us, entertained as she reminisced about her youth as a member of the choir in her church. Her only sister, Aunt Irene, always featured in her stories. Aunt Irene must have been one of the lead singers. Granny's lovely soprano voice rang out notes that wrapped around us and inspired us to join in, and one day, to become part of a choir also. Even though Aunt Irene was the younger of the two she was the obvious leader, and more adventurous. She influenced Granny to join the choir when they were teenagers.

My Walk with Christ

Having been separated from her mother and Aunt Irene when she was much younger, to go and live with her dad and stepmother, Granny had missed out on the fellowship with church and needed encouraging. She found that singing was one of her gifts, which was also cherished by the church and it brought her closer to her sister, making up for the years that they had been away from each other and her precious mother, whom she obviously treasured.

As a faithful follower of Jesus Christ, my Granny made sure that I learned and engaged with the scriptures from a very early age. Prayer is one of my most treasured memories of living with Granny. Every morning I would be awakened by her praying; she was fervent and dedicated to worshipping and honouring her Lord. She showed how much she loved her children especially, by praying for them every morning, calling out each of their full names. I would listen quietly with awe and curiosity. That's how I learned the real names of Granny's four sons and only daughter, because none of them were called by their real names by the huge number of relatives and friends that we had! My dad, whose name was Joseph, was known by everyone as Tom, or with the Jamaican twang, Tàam. Being educated at home had taken on a new twist.

Prayer was very inclusive with Granny, so I was not allowed to just be her audience. When she prayed, she always ended with the Lord's prayer and this was when I could participate. Of course when I was a toddler this was exciting and I loved praying with Granny, but as I got older my interest waned and I would curl up under the sheets, pretending to be asleep; so Granny had to insist that I get out of bed and kneel next to her each morning. At night I was reminded to pray before going to sleep. As she got to the end of her morning prayers, Granny would raise her head and say to me with urgency in her voice, "Git up ahn pray!" If I didn't move after a few minutes, she would give me a smack and repeat, "Git up ahn pray!" My prayer was always, "Our Father which art in Heaven..."

(Mathew 6:9-12),

until I became confident enough to add my own words. I remember praying to ask God for help on many occasions for different reasons, and I know He heard and answered everyone, because in most cases I received what I prayed for. I also learned that He is wiser than anyone else and loves us enough to allow some lessons to be taught through hardship.

My most frequent prayers were to remember what I had studied so I could do my best in school exams. The subjects that I gave most attention to, I always did well in, even when I wasn't feeling confident. I believe this was because I studied hard and prayed to God for help. For the subjects that I didn't make as much effort in, like maths, my marks were always low. In 2 Timothy chapter 2 verse 15, young Timothy was instructed to study the Word of God with diligence to become a qualified Minister, ordained by God to teach others in the way of truth.

Granny loved the Lord and she loved her family; all of us who have spent time with her know that she based all of her principles for living a successful life on the Words from the Bible. Learning and reciting the Psalms was one of the tools she used to teach her grandchildren and other extended family members' children about the importance of worshipping and serving the Lord God. We always felt special in Granny's presence because of how she interacted with each of us. Story times were when we would all gather around her as she relaxed in her favourite chair. We huddled together on the floor looking up at her expectantly as she silently scrolled through the long list of Anansi the SpiderMan stories, derived from African folklore and passed down through the generations of our families. Other favourites were duppy (ghost) stories; these were always full of life lessons which Granny would point out to us. I remember Bredda Anansi; he was very lazy and spent his days hanging out with his other idle friends: Bredda Tokuma, Bredda Cow and Bredda Dog. His poor wife and children had to go to work to plough the fields on the family farm while he and his friends came up with wild schemes to get easy money, which inevitably ended in disaster, because not only were they lazy, they were also cowardly and would not stand up for themselves against anyone who tried to cheat them in their easy-money schemes. They would instead squabble among themselves about who was in charge, or who deserved a greater share of profit. Bredda Anansi, who was the cleverest, always managed to wriggle his way out of the argument with more profit than the others and he would slip away before they had a chance to do anything. He didn't like sharing, even with his family; he would buy himself a large bread and eat half of it, then when he got home, dragging himself up the path breathing hard and wiping his brow with his very colourful handkerchief pretending that he had been walking a long way after a hard day's labour, he would say that half of the bread was eaten by the other men because they did not have lunch, but he brought his share home for the family. Mrs Anansi would of course feel sorry for him, so he had the other half of the bread as well!

That was such a hilarious story; imagine how fat Anansi must have been and how skinny his wife and children were! After the story and our roars of laughter and giggles had quietened down, Granny would remind us of the morals of the story. Lessons like honesty, good manners and obedience to parents, were very high priority in our moral training and their importance was not allowed to be forgotten. I believe that in her own way Granny used these stories, connected with scriptures, to teach us lessons and soften our hearts so that we would grow up to be honourable citizens filled with integrity and reverence to God.

"My child keep your father's Commandments and do not forsake the laws of your mother."

(Proverbs 6:20 slightly enhanced.)

Granny would lead us into prayerfully sing a verse of a hymn and recite Psalm 23, quietly if it was late and bedtime for those who were staying with her; she would walk the others to their door. Remembering these gatherings reminds me of the Sermon on the mount in Mathew chapters 5,6 and 7, when the Lord Jesus taught large groups of people about the principles of God's Kingdom.

Granny used her very own special proverbs and sayings as verbal guides to correct us as children. They were very mysterious and sometimes quite hilarious to us in the moment, but over time we came to recognise the subtle warnings and also to value their unique lessons that connected traditions of our grand and great grandparents. They were so embedded in my psyche that they flowed naturally to my own children.

Two of my favourite proverbs of Granny's sounded like this in Jamaican: "Debil a nyan im mumma meat im tink a bway meat." ("The devil is treating his mother's warning/correction like something his friends would say for fun.") This is saying that a child is not taking seriously the instructions of a parent, not being respectful. Before each proverbial utterance, Granny would give her head a slight shake and utter impatiently, "Aaaahhhbway," while sending us a warning look; if anyone still dilly dallied we would hear, "Fiah deh a musmus tail I'm tink a cool breeze," (a mouse will be carelessly fanning fire with his tail and think he's creating cool breeze) Ha ha, this would set us off giggling but from a safe distance. We did not wish to end up like that silly mouse!

Granny was determined that no matter what, she would do her best to make sure I always attended church and school while living with her. For this I will always be grateful to God and to her.

The love and purpose of God in our lives never fails, no matter how many times we do. For this I am truly grateful. Today I reflect back on my growing up years and instead of sorrowing over the things that I lost, or even what I wished and prayed for but never received, I will count my blessings. I will name them in recognition of God's unfailing love, faithfulness, and determination for me to succeed. The fire in His word burns in my soul, propelling me to strive so that I can thrive.

"Forgetting what's behind..."

(Philippians 2:13)

Thank you Granny. What a great start!

My Walk with Christ

A JOURNEY OF ENLIGHTENMENT

My Walk with Christ

From a tender age rocking on Granny's knee, I remember hearing her talking about God as a loving Father, who is the great and glorious Eternal Spirit who dwells in the Heavens, far beyond space and time; yet amazingly this Being, who is the one that created all things, is near enough to hear my voice and see my tears and want me to know that He loves me so much, that He sent His only son to rescue me and keep me safe for eternity. I was introduced to living transformational teachings of the gospel message: how Jesus Christ, the only begotten Son of God left His eternal glory to live and die in time for the redemption of all the people on earth, the descendants of the first Adam who rejected the perfect life of innocence and purity, and everything he and his descendants would ever need; provided for by the giver of life; not only humans but every living thing, including plants and animals, seen or unseen.

God in wisdom not only loved us when we were good in Adam's DNA, He continued to love us after Adam disobeyed His command and passed on to us his nature of disobedience, which in all its form is known as sin. Sin, or disobedience, caused the perfectly created Adam and his wife, Eve to lose their privileged position of always being close to God and having perfect lives without pain, hunger, illness or lack. God made a promise to Adam and Eve that one day a Saviour would be born who would defeat the force of evil that caused them to commit sin, and bring salvation to their descendants. Praise

God! Galatians chapter 4 verses 4, 5 and 6 talks about when the time for God's promise was fulfilled, His Son was born and His assignment to bring salvation to us was completed.

"Everyone who heard this good news would believe and confess their need for salvation and be given access to the gift of eternal life through Jesus Christ."

(John 3:16)

Granny taught me about Jesus Christ, His death, burial and resurrection; that Jesus Christ came into the world at the time that God appointed, for the purpose of bringing salvation to all people who were trapped in the enslavement of sin. He would have to bear the just punishment that every individual deserves: all are guilty, all are born sinners even though only Adam and Eve had the pre-knowledge of the outcome of disobedience. The result of their disobedience meant that over many generations people's hearts became more wicked, and disobedience to God's Laws were as easy as breathing.

God our creator continued to love humanity and give every generation opportunities to change their minds and turn back to Him in repentance, but most people kept moving away from Him. They even tried to replace Him as sovereign, by making their own ideas of how they wanted God to be. This is called worshipping of idols. Hundreds, maybe thousands of religions and beliefs have emerged from people's desires to have gods who agree with their ideas of what is good or bad, wrong or right.

Learning about the one true God, creator and keeper of all that exists on earth and beyond, sets us up for success in this life and the next. I have found that the values and beliefs that we learn in our early years are the foundations that we tend to build our lives on. We hardly ever wander very far from them, rather they become like dictionaries or maps, even counsellors that help us make decisions that define our destinies. This reminds me of the book of Proverbs, written by King Solomon, addressed to his son, filled with wise instructions and the wisdom of God so that he could have a successful life. They act like a magnet that connects life's challenges and problems with the right solutions.

Being a wise son means having an obedient and humble heart and the desire to hear the truth. An understanding heart to recognise the exceptional value of the truth and wisdom, to practice living a life of honour and obedience. Solomon, who was the wisest man who ever lived, as well as one of the richest, recognised that the greatest legacy and treasure he could pass on to his children was godly wisdom. The knowledge and understanding that to honour God in love and obedience to His laws, in this life and the next, their value and worth would surpass all the wealth in the world. Imagine having unlimited access to such wealth in today's world especially, where wealth and fame at all costs is being offered on all the social media platforms like snares for the simple mind.

"Whosoever is simple..."

(Proverbs 9:4)

"Jesus Christ, the only begotten Son of God, embodied all the characteristics of a wise Son. His mission was to be "The second Adam," who would through obedience overcome the temptation from Satan and retain His status as the beloved Son."

(Mathew 3:16-17; 4:1-11).

He was the promised Saviour, Redeemer; the Jewish Messiah or Christ (the Anointed One), promised by The Father to come and defeat the enemy and restore His people to their rightful inheritance. The Jewish people at the time of Christ's coming were in desperate need of deliverance as they were being governed by the barbaric Romans who were not believers in the God of Israel.

Thanks be to God that Jesus's mission of deliverance transcended the physical, and included all of humanity as was promised to Adam and Eve, Abraham and David. Foretold by the prophets, witnessed first by John the Baptist, the Apostles and countless others in person. In our lifetime, we too have been blessed with the opportunity to be one of His disciples!

To complete His mission, which was ultimately to purchase our lives back from the enslavement of sin, brought about by Satan (the Devil), who tricked Eve into disobeying the command of God, He had to pay the ransom price which was a human's life. Not just any human, but one that had never given in to temptation, never done, thought or said anything that could be judged by God's Law as wrong. He was pure in heart and body.

John the Baptist called Him "The Lamb of God who takes away the sin of the world."(John 1:35) That was a huge task! There John was, preaching to the large crowd of people gathered at the bank of the Jordan River, many queuing up to be baptised because they were convicted in their hearts of their sinfulness and wanted to be ready for when the Messiah that John was preaching about came, when he suddenly saw Him in the midst of the masses of people. The sign of the Spirit resting on Him was evident to John, although no one else was able to see it. John immediately stretched out his arm and shouted while looking straight at Jesus;

"Behold the Lamb of God, who takes away the sin of the world!"

(John 1:29)

"The angel told Joseph, Mary's husband and Jesus' earthly father, in a dream, that when He was born His name should be called Jesus, meaning He would save His people from their sins."

(Mathew 1:21)

Granny's constant dialogue with us about God's love for us as children, together with learning the scriptures, instilled in our hearts a deep reassurance and confidence in our worth. Even at a tender age I could feel the pulling power of the Holy scriptures as I listened to and recited them every day.

Granny never missed church services unless she or I were too ill to be there. She was truly dedicated to the service of the Lord and like Joshua in the Bible, she was faithful in all her house. Of course, this meant that any child who happened to be in her house had to also be present in every church service that she attended.

Tum tum tiddy dum, pidi di dim went the beating of the drums, as the brothers and sisters danced and weaved to the rhythm while singing traditional Jamaican gospel songs, clapping hands and knocking tambourines in joyful worship. Us little ones loved the sounds of the music; we would slowly join in clapping and singing at the top of our voices, as if competing with the adults to see who was loudest. One of Granny's favourites was, "What a wonderful thing a very wonderful thing to be free from sin and have Christ within."

The first church I remember attending with Granny was known as Mother Dawkins church on Oxford Road in the centre of Spanish Town. It was a little wooden building at the side of the road, across from the much larger New Testament Church of God, where I attended Basic school from when I was two and a half years old until I was five. We lived in a little house on this side of the road, that another elderly lady shared with Granny. We moved around quite often but Granny stayed loyal to the same church until Mother Dawkins, who was the leader, became too advanced in age and frail to continue. There were no younger members able lead, so that chapter was closed.

I still have glimpses of memory of Mother Dawkins, in the church and visiting her at home. She was taller than Granny and seemed much older with her short fluffy white hair. She looked slightly stooped when she walked; her eyes crinkled in the corners when she smiled and her voice was very soft. I still remember the feeling of happiness from being around Mother Dawkins; I felt she loved and cared for me like a member of her family. When she was unwell we visited her often, and she always called me NehNe just like Granny did.

As I got older my sense of independence emerged with a vengeance and Granny had a hard time convincing me to keep attending her home church. My reasons were that there were no young people there anymore, and it was a long way away. It felt like I had been abandoned, left alone in a strange country with strange people. We struggled to communicate, because we were now speaking different languages. This reminds me of what happened at the tower of Babel!

My Walk with Christ

After Mother Dawkins's church closed Granny needed to find another, one where their worship style was familiar to her. She met this wonderful family named Mathews when I was about eight years old. Shortly after this we moved into a rented part of their property until I turned thirteen. Two of the Mathews adult children and their families had built their houses on the property so I was surrounded by many children near to my own age. I was very happy there.

My love of sharing what I learned found many willing lives to bless! I fitted well into other people's families, playing, learning, and even eating together in the daylight. As nightfall drew near and the colours in the sky changed, each child was drawn to their own home and I went to the comfort and safety of Granny's.

Church was in a village called Church Pen, a couple of miles from Old Harbour and ten miles from Spanish Town. Every Sunday morning Granny and I travelled there by bus. We always stayed overnight with Sister Coley, a lovely quiet older lady, who was a member of the church. She became like family, always welcoming Granny and me into her lovely, beautifully kept wooden house, surrounded by fruit trees!

During the holidays we spent more time there as we didn't have to hurry back on Monday mornings for school. The long sunny days were filled with adventures; sometimes I didn't want to go back home and leave my friends who lived in Church Pen. There was an abundance of open fields to explore; all kinds of fruits: berries growing wild, mangoes hanging off the trees in easy reach for us to pick and eat, apples, plums guineps and the almost translucent favourite, jimbilin. My mouth waters just thinking of all the fresh snacks we had as children, combined with brilliant warm sunshine and the freedom to play outside all day long. The summer days seemed endless. Of course in Jamaica, the weather was mostly sunny; rain came with great gusto and excitement and then, in the blink of an eye, the sun was out again and the only reminder that it rained were the shiny droplets of water on the trees nearby, shimmering in the sun's light.

As time passed, the older teenagers drifted away one by one. I realised when I was thirteen that no one my age was there anymore; some went to other churches, others moved away and my best friend could no longer travel to Church Pen because he was playing music at a church in Spanish Town. I was heartbroken. Everyone at church were adults in their later years. I did chores for them but we didn't have many conversations.

One Sunday I decided that I didn't want to go all the way to Church Pen anymore. Granny couldn't understand why. She tried her best but couldn't convince me that day. To please her I would occasionally accompany her there, but I was lonely, with hardly any other young people around. The absence of my parents and other siblings hurt deeply, it was as if no one except Granny wanted me, and at that moment this did not feel like it was enough—except God's love and guiding hand was preparing a way. When I turned fifteen years old my understanding of repentance and remission of sins, and being born again, became clearer. . I attended a great crusade (in the big tent) with a few of my friends who lived close to the town centre where the meetings were being held. I was drawn to the electric-like charge in the atmosphere and the music. The beautiful songs from the praise team drew people from all over the city. We would almost glide around the open space close to the stage area, swaying to the music and singing along with them. The huge space was flooded with light and the flow of everything really captured my attention. Listening intently to the different preachers each night awoke my heart to a better understanding of what being a follower of Jesus Christ meant. I found myself quite separated from the friends I had before, and drawn to other young people in the church on Nugent Street (Church of God of Prophecy) near to my home, where Granny and I often attended on midweek nights.

Here I was, fifteen years old, ready to take the step of faith and surrender my life to the Lord. The crusade was over, with the safety of continued time of worship and soul inspiring preaching. I missed the pull of the comforting yet exciting sounds of the music and singing; the sense of presence of the Holy

Spirit ministering to us through words which convicted our hearts of the need to connect with the source of life, salvation and forgiveness of sins. I had prayed. I believed that God heard me, so what now? I didn't want to be baptised in Church Pen, at Granny's church. The church near to our home was where I liked to worship. Granny and I visited there regularly and enjoyed the services; furthermore lots of young people of different ages attended, even some of my uncle Ellis's in-laws. Would my Granny approve?

I spoke with a relative who was a member of the church, about my desire to be baptised. She took me to see the Pastor, who explained the procedures and requirements of becoming a born again person. I discovered that two of my friends who were at the crusade, also wanted to be baptised. I was so excited! With Granny's permission I attended the baptism classes and after two weeks, eight of us were baptised the same day. On the Sunday night we were formally given what is called 'The right hand of fellowship,' and so we became members of the Church of God of Prophecy.

I was caught in the middle of a great deal of change emotionally and physically. I was transitioning into adulthood, which made me very vulnerable and exposed to abuse from some of the most unexpected people and in places that should have been safe. I had to physically fight to protect my body from being violated on several occasions, just because I trusted an individual or because they thought I was fair game as I was alone with my Grandmother. I never told my Granny what was happening to me because I didn't want her to worry; but I was deeply affected by these experiences, which caused me to feel unsafe and angry. I realised that my attitude and behaviour must have changed dramatically, because Granny complained to my dad that I was getting difficult to live with, so he invited me to come and live with him. I know Granny continued to pray for me as always, and I was delivered from danger in moments when, without divine protection, I would have been seriously harmed. God's divine protection kept me from being harmed when threatened with danger, whether physical, mental or emotional.

We got on fairly well, my dad and me; but 'there' was not home. My dad was tall, handsome and very confident. He could see the funny side of almost any situation and had us all in stitches with his quirky jokes as soon as he saw us coming. As well as being a comedian, my dad was good at noticing things about his children, like our health, what we wore and who we associated with. He spoke his mind, sometimes really sharply, which sounded like a thunderclap in our ears; no one wanted to hang around for the possible lighting strike so we would make like a tree and leave quietly. He gave good advice about being independent and keeping healthy. I still follow some of his advice, especially about eating aloe vera (another ancient herbal remedy).

I think Granny told him to send me home after a couple months; she must have missed me as I did her. Spending time with my dad was particularly good for me as I also got to spend quality time with four of my younger siblings, making memories. My brother Steve reminded me not so long ago that I taught the four of them when they were children (in big sister's home school). I had honestly forgotten, but my heart flooded with joy when told me.

Even negative experiences serve to help us fulfill our purpose in life. My natural gifts and talents helped me to serve my family at a time when I needed them. I loved to teach. I shared what lessons I had learned in as an engaging way as possible, for maximum impact. I spent a lot of my spare time during my teens, and even preteens, honing my skills by helping children and later on, adults, to improve their reading and writing. It's as if I was on a mission to seize every opportunity for learning and sharing that came my way as if my life depended on it.

FINDING MY VOICE

Going to church on Nugent Street fitted in with my changing life in odd ways. My memories of being a part of the membership there, are mainly of the children at Sunday school; I was too old to join, so I listened and observed. I loved the songs they sang in that class, so I memorised them and later taught them to other children at other churches. I wanted so much to be able to sing like my Granny and especially aunt Irene. Aunt Irene was regularly asked to sing at a church we had attended years before. She had one of the sweetest sounding alto voices I have ever heard, before or since. She was in her sixties then. Her song was called "Hosanna to Jesus". When she stood up to sing everyone went quiet. The sound filled the building and drew us all into the warm lilting melody of the chorus.... "Sweet music sweet music with gladness we bring..."

My best experience was being accepted into the national choir at fifteen years old. I remained in the choir for two whole years until Granny and I moved house to live in a village called Featherbed Lane.

In the choir I learned the most beautiful song; which years and years later, still brought me comfort and encouragement on days when nothing seemed to be going right. "The blood that Jesus shed for me, way back on Calvary," was written by Andrè Crouch, when he was also a teenager. Being part of the combined choir did a lot for my sense of worth and confidence. I learned that I too had inherited the gift for singing and could stand alongside Granny, aunt Irene and uncle Ellis, who were my role models in how to worship, and honour God with my voice. Whenever I stood up to sing I gave it my all. God blessed me with a very strong high toned voice that rang out the melodies and blended well with other members of the choir. I felt like I was in the presence of the Holy God, expressing my thanks for the gift that I could use to praise Him!

(Psalm 13:6)

When I was sixteen years old, at the start of my final year in secondary school, an unexpected opportunity presented itself: a chance to join the Jamaica Movement for the Advancement of Literacy (JAMAL) in supporting adult learners in Spanish Town. This was a great opportunity that would add value to my young life and enable me to do what I loved. As long as I managed my time well between home and school for a few months, this would be a great success.

I was on my way to the library, one of my favourite places (as books were my dear friends), when I saw the huge banner on a government-owned building advertising for teachers. Without hesitation I went straight in and spoke with the lady who was in charge. It turned out that students were their ideal choice as this was a voluntary role. The experience would look good on our CVS too. Interacting with and supporting people with their learning always came naturally to me, so going in for two hours each day before school to teach my own class, boosted my confidence so much. I think this helped lay the foundation for me going on to starting my own basic school once all my own children were in primary school.

My time at JAMAL was very enjoyable indeed. I was able to do my two hours each day and make it to school in time for my lesson. As we got close to exam times, I had to cut back, but I never lost my enthusiasm for learning and teaching. I made a few friends who were also students, or high school graduates doing this as apprentice training before applying teacher's college. We lost touch when I moved outside of the town. I still remember some of the fun times we had. They had some video recording equipment that the technical trainees used to document some of what was being achieved in this landmark education and training endeavour. They found out that I could sing and one day were allowed to record me singing "The blood will never lose its power." That was so amazing! I had never heard myself sing before and it was such a treat. I'm so sorry I never got a copy.

I remember how deeply fulfilling it was to interact with children of different ages, imparting knowledge that they needed, and learning from them what I needed to know. My love of singing always played an important role in uniting the children and introducing new learning. One of our favourite morning songs was "Clap, clap, clap your hands, everyone together…" I think this one was made up by me: "Stamp, stamp, stamp your feet, everyone together…"

A WONDROUS REVELATION

It was on my seventeenth birthday in 1979 when Granny and I went to live on Featherbed Lane. This is where two of Granny's sons also lived. Featherbed Lane is located about five miles outside of the town centre of Spanish Town and is about two miles long. One end is on Old Harbour Road and the other on St John's Road, connecting with Job's Lane.

Moving from the centre of town to this out of the way place turned out to be the beginning of a new life for me. This is where I truly met with Jesus Christ. Where I learned what it means to "Die to Self" (my sinful nature, that is focused on thinking and doing what brings satisfaction to selfish desires that naturally contradict God's will for my life). The light (clarity) in God's words brought me on a journey to life in Christ.

Through a process of conviction, understanding the Word of God in the Bible, as was being taught by the Pastor and other leaders, my life began to change. It felt like I had been in a deep sleep and someone had gently woken me up and started to tell me about all that I had missed. My appetite was open, I felt a deep hunger in my heart to know more about walking with Christ.

The previous two years of being a member of the church in Spanish Town was good for me as it was the beginning of my journey; at this point I needed tailored support to help me prepare for the next stage of my life. I particularly needed to be away from friends whose influence would have led me further away from a close relationship with Christ Jesus.

On reflection, I realised that my Heavenly Father had made this move possible. The Lord was actually fighting for me, protecting and preserving my life so that His future plans and purpose would be accomplished, and every experience whether great or small, good or bad, would include lessons and opportunities for growth.

My first experience of church on Featherbed Lane was a bit of a culture shock. On the evening of my first Tuesday, I was invited to an Apostolic church that was near to our home. Interestingly, the Pastor lived just a few houses from ours. A few families from the church were close neighbours. I'm still in touch with these families mainly through social media, keeping the memories alive and the bond we formed strong.

Now this church building was nothing like the one I attended in Spanish Town at all. It had no walls or floor, not even a roof! Coconut boughs (leaves) were weaved by some of the young people, and used to create temporary walls. The benches were roughly carved from bits of wood. There were people of different ages scattered around the small building, making it seem larger.

My Walk with Christ

The atmosphere felt very welcoming; as I walked in, a sense of calmness and peace enveloped my mind. Youth service was going on, with lots of Bible quizzes, worship songs and sharing of testimonies. I was asked to introduce myself and testify. I told them that I was a Christian and the name of my church. For my testimony, I sang my now favourite gospel song, which would become my theme and protection song.

Here the Lord met me and gave me another chance. Here in this very humble setting, I started again. Hope was awakened in my soul. I didn't realise until much later what a meaningful beginning this was and how my decisions from that point would usher in a new era and new direction to my God ordained destiny.

The gift of singing that the Lord blessed me with in answer to my childhood prayers helped to open a new door for me in this little known place. My heart had been wounded. My life was beginning to transition; I was at the door, being invited to enter, but everything was going to have to change! Change is as continual as the seasons. I would lose everything that I trusted in, for a season, so that my future could be built in Christ Jesus.

Having just finished secondary school with what I felt was not enough qualifications or transferable skills, God's intervention was desperately needed.

My Walk with Christ

The amazing thing about God's plans and answers to our prayers are that He knows far better than we ever could what we need, when and how. At seventeen years old I needed a fresh start, a wake-up call, a challenge that was great enough to bring out of me proof that I believed in God and would be willing to walk through my life with Him.

Everything started to change from that Tuesday night. I once again sang my favourite song, " The Blood Will Never Lose Its Power". I sang this song of victory out loud with every fibre of my being, exuding confidence in my ability to deliver well. Little did I know just how much repeatedly singing this song would help to build and strengthen my faith and understanding of the love of God for all people. The passionate way I sang resulted in me being invited to sing at many church events and gospel concerts around Jamaica. Blessed to be a blessing.

In just over a month, I became a member of this little church on Featherbed Lane. On 27th July, I received the baptism of the Holy Ghost. The experience was like stepping out of time into eternity in a split second. A flood of warm light enveloped my whole being as I travelled outside of myself. Then suddenly I was back in the building, surrounded by everyone there, but I was speaking a new language and my heart was filled with a sense of peace. In that moment I made up my mind to be baptised in the Name of Jesus Christ according to the scriptures in

Act 2:38. This happened on Sunday morning, 1st August. On the same Sunday evening I sang before a large congregation at the main church in Kingston. I remember silently praying, "Lord I want to sing for you, please help me". My eyes were closed the whole time I sang. As the song finished with my little flair, I opened my eyes and saw nearly everyone was standing. The National Bishop made a fuss of me and told the congregation that I had been only baptised that morning. My Pastor had told him while I was singing. A new beginning— "Lord, take my hand".

One of my uncles had become upset with my decision to baptise again and threatened to put me out of the home. I was convicted in my heart that this was the right thing to do and went anyway, strangely unafraid. Somehow I believed that I would be alright, but how I didn't know. On Sunday after I go baptised, I told the Pastor and his wife that I couldn't go home. I went home with them and in the afternoon we went to the convocation service in Kingston. I was homeless. God honoured my faith and already had a home and family prepared to take care of me.

When I told the Pastor that I couldn't go home, he spoke to the dearest lady, who was a member of the church. Even though her house was filled with her own children, Mother (Mammy) Pike welcomed me into her family. There I stayed, except for a short while when I went back to stay at my uncles'. I was needed for that time to help Granny take care of two of my cousins. Their mum brought them to stay with their dad and he couldn't care for them and go to work. I enjoyed caring for these two boys; we really bonded and I still have a deep connection with them even though I haven't seen them in person for a long time. For a few months I was their co-carer.

This helped me to spend more time with my beloved Granny who was heartbroken because we were separated. One of my best memories of this time was Granny's Saturday Soup. She discovered a vegetable called Indian Kale, which she grew in the garden among the other foods. There were sugar canes, sorrel and gungo peas for Christmas, plus some yams called dasheen. Granny used the kale in a newly created soup that we couldn't get enough of. We all looked forward to Granny's Saturday soups and would sit at the door watching to see the ingredients that were added: bits of beef on the bone first, then vegetables like pumpkin, carrots, cho cho; later, yams and potatoes, dumplings and the now famous kale; lastly, seasoning. The bubbling soup filled the whole yard with the delicious aroma; our tummies rumbled and we would nudge each other as our mouths watered with anticipation. When the kale went in it was nearly time to eat, so we edged closer and closer until Granny would turn, smiling at us and say with a wink, "Soon done now". I can still remember the taste of Granny's Saturday soups and the joyful feeling of sharing with other family members who still remember too. There is nothing like sharing happy memories with those you love.

BEAUTIFULLY BROKEN

Life in Featherbed Lane certainly had its challenges. My return to live with Granny and my uncles didn't last. The boys went back to live with their mum, and I was perceived to be an unwelcome burden. A young adult with no income, yet. Life became rather uncomfortable so I asked Mother Pike whether it was okay to come back to stay with her. Thank God, she said yes. There I was, once again accepted as a member of the family. Nevertheless, I was eighteen years old with no job and no opportunity for going back into education; I just needed to trust in God and wait. Easier to say than do, but I learned.

I struggled to find my footing as I was used to having responsibilities, someone to take care of and connect with. I felt disconnected, at loose ends at first. It was almost impossible to see any positives. I had a special gift the Lord knew I needed in times like this, so I sang my song, in our church and in other churches where I was invited to sing. The shock of not being allowed to stay with my Granny affected me immensely; but I tried my best to remain cheerful.

I had become homeless because I decided to follow the Lord Jesus where He led me. Being welcomed into this great family without hesitation was definitely the result of God's predestination and I was and still am so very grateful. I quickly fitted into their routine, got my own chores, and there were a couple of children to keep me busy and entertained.

Not long after this I got a job at my former school, to manage and serve in the tuck shop. I really appreciated the responsibility and trust that was placed in me at eighteen years old. Five days each week for nearly one year and I learned to manage a business while serving students and staff. I was responsible for receiving and recording stock, correctly storing food, managing money and supervising staff. This wonderful little earner and boost to my confidence came to an abrupt end because of my naivety in trusting two people who in different ways, because of their influence, caused me to make some very foolish decisions; I was trapped. One day my manager called me into her office. She had a very disappointed look on her face. She very quietly asked me, " What caused you to do such a thing?" As was my usual way of dealing with shock, I didn't answer. I was also feeling guilty for my error but not brave enough to ask her what she meant, or to confess what had been happening, so she said I couldn't have my job anymore and she was very sorry. I was really sorry for letting her down, more so for losing my income, but I had to be accountable for my decisions and face the consequences.

It took me a while to recover from the loss of my integrity, the job I loved and even longer to gain the courage to stand up for myself and say no to emotional blackmail from someone I misplaced my trust in. Life is filled with lessons, many from experiences that can break our hearts, even our spirit. For those who trust in Jesus Christ, forgiveness and restoration is just a prayer away. 1 John 1:9 tells us that if we confess our sins to God in repentance (regret our actions), He is faithful to His promise and will forgive us.

Every time I felt like giving up or even when I did, the Lord would not allow me to be lost. Many times when I tried to pray, my mind would go blank, I couldn't find the right words; then I would hear the words of the song I loved to sing, as if Angels were reminding me that I did know some words about God's love. So I would close my eyes and sing until I felt peace in my heart. "The blood...that Jesus shed for me..."

Church life provided wonderful opportunities for growth and utilisation of my natural and growing spiritual skills. The leaders soon noticed that I loved teaching. I was given my own Sunday school class to manage. From there I started a youth choir. I now had children to teach all those songs that I learned at the Church of God of Prophecy in Spanish Town. Wow, I couldn't have planned that myself! With God directing our lives, no experience is wasted. I was also invited to become part of the main church choir, what a great honour that was. The children and young people welcomed the opportunity to be part of a choir with enthusiasm and passion. We grew from about five to almost twenty in just a few months. They loved learning the new songs, especially the action ones. The rhythms and movements made the words and lessons come alive in all our hearts.

Music plays such a vital role in the worship services. Skilful playing even on one instrument during the services supports the singing of hymns and choruses, and changes the atmosphere. Psalm 100 comes to mind, of entering into the Lord's presence with praise, worship and gratitude. Acknowledging His majestic power and authority; Creator, Designer Keeper and Sustainer of all people everywhere. Whose love and compassion brought life to us who were spiritually dead, because of the sin we were born with and continued to live in until, Jesus Christ came to us."

(Ephesians 2:1-6)

As the number of members increased, we were able to enclose the church building with good quality timber, add on roof and a lay a traditional concrete floor, dyed red. We could gather in the building any time and in almost every weather.

Pastor Rowe and his wife, Evangelist Rowe held regular street based services in the communities outside of Featherbed Lane. It felt like we were always going somewhere, even though we still spent most of our time in the church building; which was gradually changing structurally. We had a three week crusade in a community near to Featherbed Lane, named Willowdene. The choir sang every night; some of us lost our voices at the end. It was such an amazing experience to find myself as part of a church that went out to Minister in the wider community, just like I had experienced three years before, when I decided to start my walk with Christ.

Each night more people came and listened to the choir and the preaching of the gospel message. We felt the wonderful move of God's Spirit and saw people coming to make their own commitment to walk with the Lord Jesus Christ. At the end of the crusade, many new converts were baptised in the Name of Jesus Christ for the remission of their sins according to Acts chapter 2 verse 38. The church continued to grow as we visited different communities and held meetings where we sang worship songs, prayed for the people and our Pastor preached the gospel message of Jesus Christ.

I discovered over many years of WALKING WITH CHRIST JESUS, how painful the process of separation, transformation, preparation, purification and presentation can be for a vessel (person) that is chosen for the service of the KING. My childhood experiences, training and belief system combined to build resilience and keep me hopeful. There were many occasions when I could have given up. At times I felt isolated, a long way from even my family, during seasons of testing which have resulted in unexpected growth and discoveries of new gifts which God entrusted me with, to be used for His glory and my inner adornment. I have been BEAUTIFULLY BROKEN!

YOU CAN'T KILL PURPOSE

My heart had been transformed, strengthened, healed and protected by God, in His way. Years later I would reflect on how the presence of God in my life, His spirt and learning His words, was like an invisible ancient fortress that kept me safe from unkind words and actions that could have been devasting to my life even though most of the time I wasn't aware of it. I realised also that having been isolated from my own family, even in infancy, was pre-ordained by Jesus Christ, to prepare me for the purpose I was born to fulfil.

Sometimes I felt like I was being stripped of everything that I was, that I held dear; my friends and relatives who had been so close, were now so far away. Everything about me was becoming new. This process was painful emotionally, and lonely. I learned resilience and resourcefulness. Although my dream of going to teachers' college was never realised in Jamaica, I taught in four schools including my own. I taught in various churches, serving as Sunday school teacher, youth leader and choir director for both youth and adult choirs. God blessed and encouraged me to use my gifts wherever and whenever I was needed. My life is following the same path travelled by Abraham,

Moses, Joseph and the Apostles, even the Lord Jesus Himself, stripped of His Majesty and glory. He chose to become a human so as to bring salvation to all people. For remission of sins only sinless pure blood could do. As all of Adam's descendants are born guilty, only God could provide the perfect sacrifice. Since God is Spirit, invisible and outside of time, He had to make a new first man out of Himself to be the perfect sacrificial Lamb to be offered upon Earth on behalf of humans so that a way would be made to cleanse our consciences from the guilt of sin. Jesus Christ the Son of God became the Lamb who took away the SIN of the world.

(St. John 1:19; 3:16)

I still held on to my dream to be formally trained as a teacher after my family and I moved to England in the late 1990s. My husband Paul and I met at the little church in Featherbed Lane. He was a very powerful young Evangelist and I was a fledgling believer just learning the way in a strange place. He showed a lot of interest in my wellbeing and supported me in becoming confident to speak in front of the congregation, sharing scriptures and explaining them in simple ways so I could build up my own vocabulary. We became friends and soon realised we liked each other. I was not ready to get married at all. I wanted to go to college and get my teaching degree.

On 28th March 1981 we became Mr and Mrs White. It was a beautiful sunny day, full of love and kindness. Our families and friends helped to make our day a memorable and grand affair. We were both so young and inexperienced. We had no idea what challenges lie ahead; but God's love and mercy brought us through the tough times, the days when food was scarce, when we struggled to pay the rent, school fees and even the bus fares.

We were blessed with four wonderful children who showed immeasurable patience with our lack of money to provide nice clothes, the latest toys or birthday parties like other children had.

Petagaye was our first child, a beautiful girl with healing hands and a gentle heart. Marvena, our second, a gifted mother, teacher and friend. Then Paul Jr, the computer genius who loves numbers, and finally Nakita, the business woman, teacher and advocate. We taught them: the value of hard work and the importance of saving money, even when there is only a little; to be honest and trustworthy; to take every opportunity to learn, and that education is never wasted when taken with gratitude. Most importantly we taught our children to love God and to be His disciples. Of course Granny's proverbs still pop up with my Jamaican twang when the occasion is right!

Our little ones are all grown up now; the girls have their own families and have blessed us with eight beautiful grandchildren who all adorn our lives' journey with unconditional love, beauty, grace, hope and kindness in abundance. Two boys and six more girls: Jairobi and Maceo; Shadae, Nehema, Mariela, Naomi, Malia and Harmonie. Our family has grown and spun like a precious and beautiful tapestry, spanning three continents, cultures and skin tones. We are unbelievably rich in all that the Lord, God our Father has lavished on us.

Yes we are a family of many girls! They bring so much joy to our lives whether we see them or not. We pray for them each day, calling their names unto the Lord, committing them to His care just like my Granny did for all her children and grandchildren. I believe that the Lord Jesus honours our requests, especially when we pray according to His will.

As a family, our lives have been touched with heartbreak, shipwrecked dreams, unbelievable pain and much disappointment; but we have all experienced God's ever present help with all our needs. We are blessed with great success in our faith walk, in trusting God and learning to patiently traverse the path of trial and error and grasp the invaluable treasure in the wisdom of right choices; Proverbs 4:5-9, discovered by following the path called PURPOSE; illuminated by the Word of God, led by grace. Destination, love and peace.

When You Pray Believe

Minister Judy Creighton

My Walk with Christ

Before I became a born-again believer in Jesus Christ, I had no knowledge of what prayer was. Neither did I know how to pray. I knew about God, because my grandmother told us that we must fear God. She would say, "Pickney uno no fear God?" Today is God Day, and it is a High Day, meaning Sunday. We were not supposed to play, or make any noise on a Sunday. She would say it sternly, with an angry look on her face. That Sunday when she said it, the seed of curiosity was sown into my heart, and it made me question what kind of God could make my grandmother so angry. I was nine years old when I went on a quest to find God, but I did not come to faith until I was twenty years old. It was in the year 1982, on the first day of August, on a Sunday night when I received my water baptism, and then three months later I received the baptism of the Holy Ghost. Throughout the years, I had seen God's mighty work, and I had won many battles through prayer. Follow me on my journey and I will tell you how prayer became a powerful force in my life.

In our home we all had chores. It was my duty to tidy my grandmother's bedroom, (all her children and grandchildren called her mammy). There was a black book that always lay on her dressing table, and between the pages were wedged little bits of paper. On the front cover, golden words read: 'The Holy Bible' I was very curious about this book, and I often wondered what was the meaning of The Holy Bible?

My Walk with Christ

I never thought that the Bible was a book I should read, because I had never seen my grandparents read it, and they had never read it to us. I could read very well, and maybe, if I had read it, I would have learned about God. The only knowledge I had of His existence at that time of my life was what I heard my grandmother say about reverencing God on a Sunday. Each time I went into mammy's room to do my chore, I would hold the bible in my hands and press it close to my chest. It became like a ritual, and for some strange reason I felt a strong connection with the Bible. I found out that my grandfather, who we called dada, lived in England, and he had brought back that Bible when he returned home to Jamaica.

The Bible was not the only thing in Mammy's room that caught my attention; I was always so excited to go in her bedroom because my grandfather had also brought back a big black trunk from England, filled with many beautiful items such as: bed spreads, cutlery, plates, dresses, shoes, and handbags. I used to spend time admiring those lovely things. They were so different from what we could buy locally. My eyes had never beheld anything so desirable, so desirable that I prayed, "God, please, I would like to go to the place where these pretty things come from." Unknown to me, God heard my prayer and after twenty-seven years the Lord granted my request. There is nothing that can stop God's plan for our lives. No matter how long it takes, all we need to do is wait. In Psalms 27:14, the Psalmist

David encourages us to wait on the Lord, and be of good courage.

The opportunity came when Joshua Brooks, a bishop who was a regular visitor from England visited our church in Jamaica. One Sunday morning I entered my pastor's office to speak with him when Bishop Brooks was also sitting in there. "How would you love to come to England my dear?" he asked in a jolly way. I did not quite know what to think of his proposition, but my heart burst with joy, because just before I came into the office, I had prayed unto the Lord. I was going through some challenging situations in my marriage, which made me very unhappy. I said," Lord please take me away from these horrible situations, and Lord, I would like you to take me away from Jamaica." I accepted his offer and after a while I received an invitation to come to England. I have now lived in England for twenty-six years. When we pray, we should believe that God hears our prayer and grants our request. Even though I was a child, God heard my prayer. He said in His words,

"Suffer little children, and forbid them not, to come unto me for such is the kingdom of heaven."

(Matt 19:14KJV)

After mammy and dada died my sister Precious took possession of The Holy Bible. My sister is now deceased, and my son Donald, who went to my sister's funeral in Jamaica, brought the Bible back to

England and gave it to me. I am now the happy owner of the Bible that I had held in my hands and pressed close to my chest many years ago when I was a child. My destiny was connected to the Bible and I knew it not. For it is written,

"He that believeth and is baptised shall be saved."

(Mark 16:16)

"Delight thy self in the Lord; and He shall give thee the desires of thine heart. Commit thy way unto the Lord; trust also in Him; and He shall bring it to pass."
(Psalms 37:4-5 KJV)

God knows all things. He knows the end from the beginning. The things that are unknown to us, are known to God. One night, my sister Precious and I came home from a meeting; as we got ourselves ready to go to our bed, I heard a voice, which spoke and challenged me by asking the question, "Why don't you pray?" I thought it was my sister Precious who spoke, so I turned around and looked at her, but it was clear that she did not speak. Like the boy Samuel; when the Lord called him, he did not know the voice of the Lord as yet. So, he went in unto Eli the high priest, because he thought that it was Eli who had called him.

(1 Samuel 3:4-5 KJV)

I did not say anything to my sister, because I did not want her to think that I was hearing voices, and that I was going crazy. In obedience I knelt down at my bedside and tried to pray. It was so difficult for me to pray, because at that time I was not yet Born Again, and I did not know the voice of the Lord. I stayed in the kneeling position for a while; I felt very heavy and I became frustrated because I could not pray. I said, "I don't know how to pray, then I stood up. Although I could not pray, I was obedient. God honoured my obedience.

"If ye be willing and obedient, ye shall eat the good of the land."

(Isaiah 1:19 KJV)

We went to our bed and fell asleep. My sister and I slept in the same bed. Later into the night while we slept, a thief broke into our apartment. We were two young ladies who were sound asleep with little clothing on; we always slept like that because in Jamaica the temperature was very hot. When we woke up in the morning, we discovered that the door was open and some items were missing. My sister and I were not harmed. We were very thankful that God had sent his angels to protect us. I truly believed that if I had not obeyed the voice of the Lord and tried to pray, the outcome would be different. We should always obey God and do his will. God heard my feeble cry and sent his angels to protect us. *"The angel of the Lord encamped round about them that fear him, and delivereth them."*

(Psalms 34:7)

"He revealeth the deep and secret things: he knoweth what is in the darkness, and the light dwelleth with him."

(Daniel 2:22 KJV)

Prayer is the master key that can open any iron gate. Prayer will summon angels to come to our rescue. The Apostle Peter was shut up in prison, *"But prayer was made without ceasing by the church unto God for him."*

(Acts 12 5,10 KJV)

God sent his angel and delivered him. Peter walked out through an iron gate that open on its own accord.

Gaberial the Angel was sent to deliver the answer to Daniel. Daniel prayed for twenty-one days. God heard his prayer from the first day (Daniel 10:2,12). The devil tried to block the answer getting back to Daniel, but he was persistent in prayer until the answer came. We should preserver in prayer until we get our answer from the Lord. When trouble arises in our lives , prayer is the weapon we should use to conquer the attacks of the enemy. I believe that God listens to all our conversations. He is our present help in trouble. Without prayer my life would be filled with uncertainty. Prayer gives me strength and increases my faith so that I am able to bear fiery trials.

And we know that all things work together for good to them that love God, to them who are the called according to His purpose.

(Romans 8:28 KJV)

I have faced many challenges in my life. Depression is one which I have dealt with. It made me feel anxious and afraid. I could not go outside of my house. When I ate anything, I brought it back up; I slept most of the time and I did not want to take my bath; sadness overwhelmed me and all I could do was pray. The Lord heard my prayer, and He gave me some instructions which were: "Get up! Take a shower, put on your best clothes and go into town and shop!" I obeyed and my health was restored. I went to Church that night dressed up in my finest clothes. I felt very important, like an ambassador. After the service was over, one of the Elders of the church came to me and he said, "Sis Creighton, I did not know that it was you! I was wondering, who was that beautiful lady sitting in front of me? All through the service I kept wondering, who is that person? You looked so elegant."

The Elder's remark made me realise that God's way is unsearchable, and that His way is the right way. Again, I would like to say that to obey God is the highest sacrifice that we can give to him. It shows that we trust and believe His word. The bible says: *"That God honour his word above his name."* (Psalms 138:2 KJV)

We should take time to acquaint ourselves with the Lord. It is not possible to maintain a close relationship with the Lord without spending quality time with him. My concept of God is crucial to my relationship with him. I believe that God the Creator exists; I have come to trust and believe in him. He has been ever consistence. Everything will fail; such as money, education, house and land, car, anything, but Jesus never fails. We should pray with expectation. The Holy Spirit is our helper, he wants to hear from us. He will hold out his royal sceptre of love, and bid us to come near unto him.

Those who have unanswered prayers, could become doubtful and discouraged. You should not lose sight of hope and always view the cup of life as half full. When my sister Precious died, I had personally found that holding on to hope has helped me stay on course during the time of bereavement. Before she died, I told her that I was writing my book, and that I had dedicated it to her. Through consistent prayers God gives me strength to stay focused during those sad times.

We are always to pray and not to faint. God is listening. We should pray in faith and trust and obey his word. The Lord is able to supply all our needs. Prayer is like the royal telephone that allows us to talk to Jesus almost anytime. The Lord is never too busy to hear your request. The bible says *"Behold, the eye of the Lord is upon them that fear him, upon them that hope in his mercies."* (Psalms 33:18 KJV)

My Walk with Christ

Prayer is a gift that God has given to us. Therefore, I have an advantage, and special right, with immunity, because we are God's peculiar person. What a privilege it is to take my troubles to the Lord in prayer. It gives me great joy to know that the Lord understands, and that he can be touched with the feelings of my sufferings. Prayer changes things and could change any difficult situation, so I pray in the good times and in the bad times, so when troubles come into my life, I am already equipped with strength, and by faith I face my challenges with confidence. I remember the times when I did not pray, because I did not believe, and I was afraid that God would not hear me. Disobedience produced fear. Since I had surrendered my life to Jesus, I found courage and I replaced fear with confidence, and now I come boldly to God's grace. God knows how to deliver us in times of trouble.

If we need strength God will give us difficulties, to make us strong,

God will give us problems to solve, to make us wise.

God will give us danger to overcome, so we can have courage.

"The righteous cry, and the Lord heareth, and delivers them out of all their troubles."

(Psalms 34:17KJV)

"When we pray, we should enlarge our asking capacity, and make our request reasonable and

practical. The Lord wants us to ask largely and abundantly, because He has the answers."

God's love and his ability to provide has given me the experience to know that I can depend on Him. I was a single mother with one son. I never had enough to take care of him. Life was very hard. Many times my son and I experienced hunger and I could not provide for his basic needs. Every day was a struggle just to make ends meet. I prayed unto the Lord these words, I said, "Lord, please send help." Then one night while I was at church, one of the mothers of the church came to me, her name was sis Daisey Scott. She told me that while she was at her home praying, the spirit of the Lord spoke to her heart and said, When you cook, remember sis Creighton because she is in need." Creighton is my maiden name. Since that time mother Scott brought food every Thursday for my son and I. Thursday was the day of fasting for the church. I would make sure to be at church each Thursday to receive the provision that God had made for us. Like Elijah, when God told him to arise and get to Zerephat where provision was made for him.

(1 Kings 17: 9)

For weeks I could not pay my rent; when the Landlord came to collect it, he would threaten me with eviction. It was an embarrassing situation. I would ask for more time, and he took pity on me and gave me more time to pay. I believe that God gave me favour by softening his heart. I had also received help from my mother Carmen Cox, who is now deceased. She came to my aid and gave me money to pay my rent. One of my fellow tenants tried to get me evicted because he wanted my apartment to be given to one of his relatives. He gave cigarettes and alcohol to the landlord to influence him. One day, while I was sitting inside my apartment reading my bible, I heard them weaving their wicked plot against me. I fasted, and I prayed unto the Lord; he heard my prayers and overturned their evil scheme. I heard no more talk of eviction, and I continued to live in that apartment for a long time, until I got married and moved away.

The responsibility to take care of my son was great. My only source of income was from doing odd jobs such as washing and ironing. When I went to work, my employer gave me so many clothes to wash and iron, it appeared as if she had also included her neighbour's clothes. I worked very diligently because I needed money to provide enough food to feed my son. My wages were very small compared to the amount of work I had to do. I did not complain, fearing that I would be dismissed, so I continued to endure the hardship.

I started early in the morning and worked until late in the evening. One morning, as I stood over the ironing-board with the iron in my hand, I looked at the very huge bundle of clothes, sighed deeply and shook my head from side to side. I knew that all help for me comes from the Lord, and I had committed

My Walk with Christ

myself in fasting and prayer which helped me to develop spiritual strength and increase my faith in Jesus Christ. I felt the anointing of the Holy Ghost come upon me, and a righteous anger rose up in my spirit, then I prayed unto the Lord. I said, "Lord it is not fare! Let my employer pay me more money for my services, because it's worth more."

I will never under estimate the power of fasting and prayer. The same day, after I had prayed, my employer came to me and she said, "Judy I am going to raise your pay." She also promised that she would provide lunch for me each day that I came to work. Praise the Lord, hallelujah! I felt in that moment as if I had conquered the city of Jericho! She kept her promise. She raised my pay and provided lunch for me.

"Small is the new big when our faith is in God. If you need a miracle, you will get a problem." (J C)

"Be careful for nothing, but in everything by prayer and supplication with thanks-giving make your request be made known unto God." (Philippians 4:6KJV)

We should never be discouraged. God is always present. He never misses an appointment. When Adam sinned in the Garden of Eden, he did not show up for his appointment, because he was afraid (Genesis 3:10). But God was waiting for him there. God is never late. Jesus is our present help in trouble. God is my provider and He is my healer.

My Walk with Christ

For many years I had suffered with migraine headaches; I thought that I would have to live with this condition for the rest of my life. I never knew that healing was available to me. One night when I was experiencing a severe headache I went to church. My head was throbbing, I was in agony. I heard from the preacher for the first time that I could be healed. I believed, and that same night I was healed from the spirit of migraine headaches. This happened over forty years ago and it has never come back. That healing experience had re-enforced my commitment to walk with Christ.

It gives me great joy and it's a pleasure to come boldly unto the Lord in time of need. I have wonderful peace knowing that Jesus cares for me. I can truly say that the joy of the Lord is my strength. Despite the dark clouds, the boisterous wind and the storms that blew into my life, I had continued to go forward, trusting in the Lord. I am determined that whenever I go through suffering, I will endure it to the end. I will never give up on God. He promised to take me safely to my destination on the other side.

Therefore I stand upon the promises of God's word, in which He has made provision whereby we can be sustained. There is no problem too big for God to solve . There is no mountain so high that God cannot move it. He is the resurrection and the life. He can resurrect our dreams that were dead. He certainly has resurrected my dream of becoming an author.

Today my dream is alive, and I am pressing forward towards my goal.

"Man shall not live by bread alone but by every word that proceeds out of the mouth of God."

(Matthew 4:4)

There is no warning when trials and trouble come knocking at our door. Jesus teaches that we should watch and pray so that we will not be afraid. When we pray, we should believe that the Lord will make a way of escape for us, and that it will be well.

Fear was one of my biggest challenges. It killed my dreams and it prevented me from trusting in the Lord. It was a barrier which stopped me from developing a strong relationship with the Lord Jesus Christ. Fear overwhelmed me and my life was plagued with unbelief. I had no confidence in the Lord. In my arrogance, I blamed God for all my troubles. In my pride I said, "God, you know what I need, why are you not blessing me?" This is the answer that the Lord gave to me. He said, "You have nothing, because you fight for nothing." I was shocked when I heard the answer that God gave to me. I could not think positively. I had no hope. Fear imprisoned my mind and my unbelief was an addiction which numbed my soul. An eerie shadow was cast upon my path. I could not see my way out.

For many years I had suffered inside myself. No one knew how afraid I was. I was terrified and I had lost all my confidence. I never felt that I was good enough. I always felt that I would never mount to anything good or could ever achieve success. I was weak but God is strong. The Word of God said, "Let the weak say, I am strong." (Joel 3: 10 KJV)

I was inspired by the Word of God, and a new spirit of courage and hope rose up inside my soul, and I broke free from the spirit of bondage. Despite all my efforts, I could do nothing without Christ. But when I prayed to the Lord, seeking, asking and knocking, Jesus heard my cry. He gave me power to love myself and to overcome the spirit of fear. Courage is the opposite of fear, so I encourage myself in Jesus and Keep on trusting in him. The Word of God renewed my mind, and the love of Christ has taken me to new heights. I understand that I have worth. I value myself, because I am worthy to be loved.

God does not give us the spirit of fear, but of power and of love and of a sound mind. (2 Timothy 1:7 KJV)

Courage is that you are the only one who knows that you are afraid.

"Faith and persistence not only determine your victory, but also the extent to which you win." (J.C)

My Walk with Christ

Here is a poem that I wrote, to remind us that we should not forget to pray:

Pray Always

We should not forget to pray

Today your faith will not delay

Be strong and be of good courage

On Christ cast all your worries

Take your troubles to the Lord in prayer

For you are inspired by the Holy Ghost fire

Jesus is listening he hears your cry

Your request he will never deny.

Beauty in Humility

When I was a child, my relatives believed that my sister Precious was more beautiful than I. I remembered how everyone would shower her with their love. On Sunday evenings my aunties would dress her in beautiful clothes and put bright coloured ribbon in her hair and they would take her for walks, but they would leave me behind. My sister was undeniably beautiful; she was a very happy girl and had great self-confidence.

I was a very shy and frightened little girl and I was an introvert. I was quiet, very reserved and always caught myself lost in thoughts. I lacked confidence, so I always looked down to the ground. I was never jealous of my sister, but I felt sad, and I wished that my relatives would shower me with love also.

I never complained. I found a unique way to encourage and comfort my heart. I was born with twelve fingers and every time they took my sister for a walk, I would look at my fingers and tell myself that I was very special and unique. According to Psalms 139: 14, *"I am fearfully and wonderfully made."*

I was the one that they would ask to run errands and render services such as washing, cooking and cleaning. I had never refused, and I committed myself to their request with humility and obedience . I believed that my obedience made me stand out from the rest of my siblings and appear beautiful to them, they could always rely on me. I believe that there is beauty in humility, which is the mark of holiness.

Even though they favoured my sister, I continued to serve with excellence and humility.

Since I became a born-again believer in Jesus Christ, and had studied the Word of God, I had grown in the grace and love of Jesus Christ. Now I understand that suffering and rejection is a part of God's humbling process.

Humility precedes honour. The way up is the way down. Humility is the posture that we should take when we walk with Christ. Humility produces fruitfulness. It is by believing and trusting in the Lord that we are able to know the Will of God for our own lives . Suffering is a process that we should go through; it helps to develop the beauty of the spirit of humility within us. Jesus demonstrates how beautiful it is to be humble. I read in the scriptures:

"He was led as a lamb to the slaughter, and a sheep before his shearers, was dumb, so he openeth not his mouth."

(Isaiah 53:7 KJV)

"When he was reviled, reviled not again; when he suffered, he threatened not; but committed himself to him that judgeth righteously."

(1 Peter 2: 23 KJV)

"The premium of humility is high, buy today the returns will be great." (J C)

"Though he were a son yet learned he obedience by the things which he suffered." (Hebrews 5:8 KJV)

Without humility I would never have been able to grow, develop or mature into a strong believer in the Lord Jesus Christ. I learned to be humble through suffering. Walking with Christ gives me hope, and He assures me that He will never leave me nor forsake me. When the way gets dark, I break free from natural thinking. I rise up in faith and put my trust in the Lord. My active communication with God gives me dynamic authority over fear and doubts.

The Wordsworth dictionary definition for humble is to show a modest or low estimation of one's importance, or to come from an unprivileged background.

I believe that humility has a deeper meaning, and it is a virtue which pays great dividend.

It can exalt us into a place of power. To stay exalted we need to be obedient, and remain submissive unto God the Creator. It is written that if we exalt ourselves we shall be abased, but if we humble ourselves we shall be exalted (Luke 14:11). We must remain faithful, with a teachable heart. Humility is a virtue; I learned over the years that to be humble is not how I feel, but it is how I believe. In the Bible the story is told of a man named Abraham. He walked with God, and believed His word, and it was accounted unto him for righteousness (Genesis 15:6).

"Humility is persevering when you are overlooked and rejected." (J C)

Once when I prayed, it felt like someone held me by my collar and lifted me up from off the ground. Then the Lord spoke to me. He said," Come Up Higher!" I was not sure if I was dreaming or if I was in a trance. Then He said to me, "Go and do," but before I heard what I should go and do, I said, Lord, "I can't do it". He was wroth and in a very stern voice He said, "Go down!" I woke up out my trance and I was afraid. I did not understand what the Lord meant when he told me to go down, I thought that I had missed my opportunity for an exceptional blessing. I could not be contented so I fasted and prayed. I asked the Lord to reveal to me what he meant when he said, "Go down!"

After a few weeks the Lord gave me the meaning. He said, "The meaning of the dream is 'The way up is the way down', humble yourself." According to 1 Peter 5:6, Peter tells us to humble ourselves under the mighty hand of God, that he may exalt us in due time. I came to understand that the Lord's concept of humility, is different from man's concept.

I still did not understand what it meant to be humble. I thought to myself, where can I find the best concept of humility according to God's concept? I believe that the Bible is the Word of God, so I researched the word 'humble' in the Bible and I found the verses of scriptures which say:

"And been found in fashion as a man he humbled himself, and been obedient unto death, even the death of the cross." (Philippians 2: 8)

"Wherefore God also hath highly exalted Him, and given Him a name which is above every name." (Philippians 2: 9)

Now I understand that Jesus Christ is our perfect example of humility, and that being obedient through suffering means being exalted. Suffering is required to be taken with grace and patience. God, in his love and wisdom makes us humble through suffering, so that we might progress and have good success.

"Transformation is a process; change is not always welcome." (J C)

"And he humbled thee, and suffered thee to hunger, and fed thee with manna, which thou knew not, neither did thy fathers know; that He might make thee know that man doth not live by bread alone, but by every word that proceeds out of the mouth of the Lord doth man live." (Deuteronomy 8:3 KJV)

My Walk with Christ

Count The Cost

Walking with Christ can be an adventure. An adventurer is one who takes risks in the hope of gaining experience. We may never know what we might encounter when we embark on our journey. Therefore it is wise to count the cost. Words such as: joy, peace, contentment, good, success, blessings and so on, are used to paint a beautiful picture of the life of a believer. But like roses that are not without thorns, life is not without trouble. Those who are enlisted in the army of the Lord know that self- denial is required to serve the Lord. We should take daily inventory to make sure that we have what we need for our journey.

"And he said unto them all, if any man will come after me, let him deny himself, and take up his cross daily, and follow me." (Luke 9:23 KJV)

When I made my vow and decided to walk with Christ, it was because of my first impression of Him. I made my decision based on God's love, which I had experienced. One day, when I was eighteen years of age, I came home from my job and sat down. I began to think about my day's accomplishments; my thoughts turned and I reflected on my life, and I was not satisfied; I had made little to no progress. I became pregnant at a very young age, and I dropped out of school. I was a single mother with no education and my future looked bleak. I thought deeply about my life and I felt like a failure. I was overwhelmed with sadness, and I fell into a deep depression. It felt like the whole world was on top of me, pressing me down. It was one of the darkest days of my life.

I was always a happy young woman and this was a different kind feeling; it made me very uncomfortable. As I sank deeper into this abyss of darkness and fear, I heard a voice which said to me, "Remember what they say, that when you have problems you should smoke weed." I was not a weed smoker, but at that time I would have done anything to get the weight up off me. I went and got the weed. I locked myself in my bedroom and smoked about four joints.

Before I finished smoking all four joints I felt like everything was spinning. It was all spinning so fast and out of control. That was not the result that I had expected. That was a set-up and the plan of Satan to make my life spiral out of control into the pit of shame and regret. The same voice spoke to me and said, "If this does not work you will have to try something harder." I knew what it meant, and I was willing to try anything to escape the demons that wanted to possess my soul. The devil is a liar and a deceiver. He deceived Adam and Eve in the Garden of Eden. He is still deceiving the human race today.

But God came to my rescue. He told me to look in the mirror, there were mirrors on the headboard of my bed. As I looked, I saw my face change into about ten ugly faces. The voice of Jesus spoke, he said to me, "You are very ugly, but do not worry, you will

My Walk with Christ

become very beautiful, and someone will come and rescue you." I looked and I saw a beautiful face appear. Then I saw a hand come down out of the clouds; He held me close, very tenderly, and embraced me in his loving arms. I had never felt such sweet love. He calmed me with his peace, and hope for the future sprang up in my soul. All my fears subsided, everything was stilled, and the weight of depression was lifted. I cried for joy. That wonderful experience helped me to make the decision to walk with Christ.

"The measure of a man is not who he is in the time of convenience, but who he is in time of conflict." (Martin Luther King)

God's love is so sweet. It's the kind of love that keeps you holding on, you can never get enough. It gets sweeter and sweeter as the days go by. God's love is like a burning fire deep down in my soul. I build my faith upon the foundation of God's love and I am determined never to turn back from following the Lord.

But how could I have known the challenges that await me on my journey, as I walk with Christ?

"Where there is faith there is obstacle." (J C)

One of the earliest experiences I had was while I was in church one day and I heard the voice of the devil. He whispered and appeared charming, but I came to find that his words were like a drawn sword. The first Sunday I attended church after I was baptised in water, I was very happy and felt a freedom that I had never known before, believing that I had made the right decision to walk with Christ. As I sat and listened to the pastor preach, the sermon seemed dynamic and as though every word was directed towards me. But before I had time to process what had been said, the devil made his move on me. He challenged my commitment with a question. He asked me, "Did you know that you will have to come to church every day?" The devil continued to test my faith, and used my pride against me. He said to me, "Do not worry, you are not too bad, because you have never killed anyone."

The devil realised that the Word of God was having a positive impact on me, so he tried to sow seeds of doubt and discouragement into my heart. My heart was already filled with many negative thoughts but I was at the right place to get the Word of God, which was the medicine that my soul needed for it to be healed. My heart was like an abscess, hard and painful. The devil did not want to lose control of my life. I was just a new born babe in Christ, and I needed the sincere milk of the Word of God to help me to grow up strong in the Lord, and in the power of his might. My mind was underdeveloped so I did not have sound judgement. In that moment I thought about what he said, and I felt very comfortable with myself.

Pastor continued to preach the word with the anointing and the power of the Holy Ghost. Then I felt like something pierce my heart, and it broke. It felt like corruption leaked out, and my spiritual eyes were opened. I realised that I was not innocent, and that I needed to repent.

Repentance is the breaking of the heart.

I said, "Lord please forgive me, I did not know that I was so wicked, I will serve you, even if it takes going to church every day and night." There were always activities at church. I wanted to be involved so I went to church every day of the week. The devil's fear of me becoming aware of who I was came to pass, and I became the devil's greatest nightmare. The devil is a liar and a deceiver but the Word of God triumphs over his lies. It's been over forty years since I made the decision to walk with Christ. The Word of God taught me how to be strong and stay focused as I continue on my walk with Christ.

"But the Word of God is quick and powerful, and sharper than any two-edged sword, piercing even to the dividing asunder of soul and spirit, and of the joints and marrow, and is a discerner of the thoughts and intents of the heart."

(Hebrews 4:12 KJV)

Nothing becomes truly great until it overcomes something that looks insurmountable. Great doors of opportunity always come with great challenges, and each challenge calls for greater faith and tenacity. I chose to despise the shame and endure the pain, and take up my cross daily and follow

Jesus. Surrendering to God is not weakness, it's wisdom. I no longer see a molehill as a mountain. So when the night comes, and the way is dark, and I cannot see any light at the end of the tunnel, I will not be afraid, as long as Jesus walks beside me.

"Big is not in numbers, it is in my faith. Faith works in the realm of impossibility." (J C)

Where he leads me, I will follow for I have learned to trust and believe in his unconditional love. Here is a poem that I wrote of God's wonderful love.

Potent Love

When you are in love, life has new meaning,

When you are in love, life's worth living,

When you are in love, your heart seems to skip a beat,

When you are in love, the shadows are so sweet.

I keep falling in love with Jesus,

I enjoy spending time with him,

alone in prayer.

Some of my family and friends thought that I was weird. They could not understand my devotion to the Lord, and along the way I lost some friendships. I had counted the cost and I kept going forward. Today, after forty years, I am nearer home than when I first began. I wrote a poem for those who despised and rejected me. Also, for those people who gave me six months to quit serving Jesus.

The Power of God's Love

Except you are connected to this power of love

You could never be the one for me

Oh, baby can't you see, God's love will set you free.

Except you are connected to this power of love

Our coming together could never be

Oh, baby can't you see, God's love will give you victory.

Except you are connected to this power of love

You'll miss God's possibilities

Oh, baby can't you see, God's love will give you liberty.

Believe Versus Unbelief

"Lord, I believe help thou my unbelief." (Mark 9:24 KJV)

A missionary once came to witness to me about Jesus. He told me that Jesus was crucified on the cross of Calvary, and that Jesus died so that I could live. The missionary led me into prayer, he called it the sinner's prayer. I prayed the prayer with him out of respect for the guy. I never understood what the prayer meant. He asked me if I believed that Jesus died to save my soul. I said yes, I believe. The missionary was happy. He was so happy he laid down on the floor with his hands and feet up in the air! He said, "Thank God you are saved." In my heart I did not believe, so when he left I said, "What an idiot, telling me that I am saved." I said, "Save what? I am still the same person, I see no change."

I put what he had told me out of my mind and continued with my life as it was. It was unknown to me that I had made a confession with my mouth and although my heart was not in agreement, God heard.

Two weeks after I had prayed with the missionary, I had a visitation from the Lord. The Lord challenged me again by asking me a question, "Did not that man tell you that you are saved?" The voice seemed to come from behind so I spun around to see who it was, but there was no one behind me. "That's strange," I said to myself. Then I answered, "Yes, he told me that I was saved, but I am still the same person." Then he asked, "So, what are you going to do about it?" I knew then I had to make a decision. So, from that day up to now, I had made the choice to walk with Christ. I had counted the cost, and I had been through many dangers, toils and smears, and not looked back.

My Walk with Christ

No one told me that the journey would be easy, but when I believe God's word, I have victory.

His promises are sure. In him we live, in him we have our being. God cannot lie. There is only one liar and deceiver, the devil, and he is the father of lies; he is like a roaring lion seeking who he may devour. We are like pilgrims just travelling through. He uses all kinds of distractions to lure us away from the right path. The story of the pilgrim progress, written by John Bunion is a good example of how the devil used distractions to lure weary pilgrims away from holiness, into a life of sin. To believe God is to believe the promises, because God's word always accomplishes that which it sets out to do. Not to believe God is prideful and God sees the proud from far off. God always prepares us for our journey. He gives us his word for instruction and for guidance.

As a new born babe in Christ, I needed support and guidance; the sincere milk of God's word that I desire, has given me strength and wisdom. I have learned how to discern differences pertaining to right or wrong, light or darkness. The face of evil sometimes appears as light. In every challenging situation I stand upon the promise of God's word. God honours His word above his name. It is a very terrible disrespect to doubt God's word. I have learned from the Word of God that those who despise God's words, suffer consequences.

"For what if some did not believe? Shall their unbelief make the faith of God without effect?" (Romans 3:3 KJV)

God Supplied Needs

All our needs God has already supplied. Like every father who knows how to give good gifts to his children, God, who is our heavenly father, knows more how to provide good gifts for us, his children. He wants us to come to him and ask him for what we need. Sometimes, when we do not activate our faith in God's word, we rather rely on man. When I was going through a crisis, I had made that mistake, of putting my trust in man, because when the challenges of life came knocking at my door, I had ignored my privilege to take my problems to God in prayer first.

Once when I was faced with some fiery trials, my needs became so great, like a mountain. I saw no way of how I could break through. Any kind of help that I got would be appreciated. I went and asked a friend for help. My friend was not very happy that I had asked him for help so he angrily shoved a twenty dollar note into my hand and said, "Do not do it again." I was so embarrassed I cried. I prayed unto the Lord. I said, "Lord did you see how my friend treated me? Did you hear what he said to me?" The Lord answered and said,

"Serves you right, why did you go and ask him? When you need anything come and ask me first. The Lord chasten the son He love." (Hebrews 12:6 KJV)

From that time up to now, I have not made it a habit to ask anyone for help before I ask the Lord first. When I ask the Lord for help first, he always provides for me, through the people who he chooses to supply my needs.

"But my God shall supply all your need according to his riches in glory." (Philippians 4:19 KJV)

If I should write about all that the Lord has done for me, this book could not hold all the contents.

"There is a need that we all have. We all have need of a saviour. For God so loved the world that He gave His only begotten Son, that whosoever believeth in Him should not perish, but have everlasting life." (John 3:16 KJV)

Jesus Christ is the source of our life. He is the God of all flesh. I love the Lord; in Him I have eternal life. In Him I have joy, peace and hope. His sweet, pure and unconditional love keeps me satisfied.

Praise the Lord! Thank you Jesus.

My Walk with Christ

Motivating Scriptures

Pastor Neruka White

Love bears all things [regardless of what comes], believes all things [looking for the best in each one], hopes all things [remaining steadfast during difficult times], endures all things [without weakening]. Love never fails [it never fades nor ends]. But as for prophecies, they will pass away; as for tongues, they will cease; as for the gift of special knowledge, it will pass away. For we know in part, and we prophesy in part [for our knowledge is fragmentary and incomplete]. But when that which is complete and perfect comes, that which is incomplete and partial will pass away. For now [in this time of imperfection] we see in a mirror dimly [a blurred reflection, a riddle, an enigma], but then [when the time of perfection comes we will see reality] face to face. Now I know in part [just in fragments], but then I will know fully, just as I have been fully known [by God].

- 1 Corinthians 13:7-10, 12 AMP
  https://bible.com/bible/1588/1co.13.7-12.AMP

- **Today I am grateful for:**
  1. The power in the depth, height and breadth of God's love in his work for all human beings that will never fail.

2. The call to worship the one true God!
Almighty Saviour, healer, deliverer and communicator in every language under the sun. The One who KNOWS EVERYTHING yet still LOVES EVERYONE without partiality. The only distinction is: belief/faith and unbelief/lack of faith
3. The power of choice.

- **Today I am grateful for:**
  1. Life, filled with purpose and hope!
  2. My family being healthy and in good spirits
  3. The growth and strength of the fellowship of CJCA Leeds. For how God is using the sharing of natural food to help us prepare for the abundance of spiritual food that we will be sharing!

  Today I will, by God's grace give help and support to our volunteers at NSK.
  Help and pray for those who come to us for food etc.
  Check on the brethren.

  Thank you Lord for your blessings and challenges on this day. Please be with us. Guide us with your eyes. Lead us not into temptations but deliver us from all evil. We are your people and the sheep of your pastures. Your Kingdom come oh Lord, your will be done on earth as in Heaven. Amen.

- *"Whatever job you're given to do, do it. God is with you!"* (1 Samuel 10:7, MSG)5

Three things that I am grateful for today:

1. God has chosen me and placed His Spirit in me. His Spirit gives me power, love and a sound mind.

-

2. I can and will fulfil my purpose, by prioritising my time, my actions, my thoughts. I will encourage myself in the Lord and choose people with integrity to hold me accountable, so that I can refocus whenever I lose track.

-

3. I have wisdom from the Lord and the ability to be a great leader. God chose me and placed in me the ability, passion, insight and knowledge to accomplish His good plan and purpose for my life and those whose lives mine will impact.
For the glory of God.
Lord I believe. 8/9/2020

"Then the word of the LORD came unto me, saying: Before I formed thee in the belly I knew thee; and before thou camest forth out of the womb I sanctified thee, and I ordained thee a

prophet unto the nations. Then said I, Ah, Lord GOD! behold, I cannot speak: for I am a child. But the LORD said unto me, Say not, I am a child: for thou shalt go to all that I shall send thee, and whatsoever I command thee thou shalt speak. Be not afraid of their faces: for I am with thee to deliver thee, saith the LORD. Then the LORD put forth his hand, and touched my mouth. And the LORD said unto me, Behold, I have put my words in thy mouth. See, I have this day set thee over the nations and over the kingdoms, to root out, and to pull down, and to destroy, and to throw down, to build, and to plant."
(Jeremiah 1:4-10 KJV)
https://bible.com/bible/1/jer.1.4-10.KJVThe

"The LORD is my shepherd; I shall not want. He maketh me to lie down in green pastures: He leadeth me beside the still waters. He restoreth my soul: He leadeth me in the paths of righteousness for his name's sake."
(Psalm 23:1-3 KJV)

"And the LORD answered me, and said, Write the vision, and make it plain upon tables, that he may run that readeth it. For the vision is yet for an appointed time, but at the end it shall speak, and not lie: though it tarry, wait for it; because it will surely come, it will not tarry."
(Habakkuk 2:2-3 KJV)
https://bible.com/bible/1/hab.2.2-3.KJV

https://bible.com/bible/1/psa.23.1-3.KJV

Minister Judy Creighton

Romans 8:20 (KJV)
For the creature was made subject to vanity, not willingly, but by reason of him who hath subjected the same in hope.

Galatians 4:18 (KJV)
But it is good to be zealously affected always in a good thing, and not only when I am present with you.

Colossians 2:7 (KJV)
Rooted and built up in him, and stablished in the faith, as ye have been taught, abounding there in with thanks-giving.

1 John 3:22 (KJV)
And whatsoever we ask, we receive of him, because we keep his commandments, and do those things that are pleasing in his sight.

1 Peter 5:6 (KJV)
Humble yourselves therefore under the mighty hand of God, that ye may exalt you in due time:

Ephesians 5:19 (KJV)
Speaking to yourselves in psalms and hymns: and spiritual songs, singing and making melody in your heart to the Lord;

My Walk with Christ

James 4:7(KJV)
Submit yourselves therefore to God. Resist the devil, and he flee from you.

1Corinthans 1:25 (KJV)
Because the foolishness of God is wiser than men and the weakness of God is stronger than men,

James 1:5(KJV)
If any of you lack wisdom, let him ask of God, that giveth to all men liberally, and up braideth not; and it shall be given him.

2 Timothy 3:16(KJV)
All scripture is given by inspiration of God, and is profitable for doctrine, for reproof, for correction in righteousness;

Proverbs 15:4(KJV)
A wholesome tongue is a tree of life: but perverseness therein is a breach in the spirit.

Proverbs 16:9(KJV)
A man's heart deviseth his way: but the Lord directed his steps.

Proverbs 22:4(KJV)
By humility and the fear of the Lord are riches, and honour, and life.

Proverbs 19:15(KJV)

Slothfulness casteth into a deep sleep; and an idle soul shall suffer hunger.

Proverbs 28:26(KJV)
He that trusteth in his own heart is a fool: but whoso walketh wisely, he shall be delivered.

Proverbs 13:20 (KJV)
He that walketh with wise men shall be wise; but a companion of fools shall be destroyed.

Philippians 3:14 (KJV)
I press toward the mark for the prize of the high calling of God in Christ Jesus.
Psalms 23:1 (KJV)
The Lord is my Shepherd I shall not want.

Psalms 46:1 (KJV)
God is our Refuge and Strength, a very present help in trouble.

Psalms 62:8 (KJV)
Trust in Him at all times; ye people; pour out your heart before Him: God is a Refuge for us.

My Walk with Christ

Inspiring Poetry Corner

"I will lift up mine eyes unto the hills, From whence cometh my help. My help cometh from the LORD, Which made heaven and earth. The LORD is thy keeper: The LORD is thy shade upon thy right hand. The sun shall not smite thee by day, Nor the moon by night."
(Psalm 121:1-2, 5-6 KJV)
https://bible.com/bible/1/psa.121.1-6.KJV

"For a small moment have I forsaken thee; but with great mercies will I gather thee. In a little wrath I hid my face from thee for a moment; but with everlasting kindness will I have mercy on thee, saith the LORD thy Redeemer. For the mountains shall depart, and the hills be removed; but my kindness shall not depart from thee, neither shall the covenant of my peace be removed, saith the LORD that hath mercy on thee."
(Isaiah 54:7-8, 10 KJV)
https://bible.com/bible/1/isa.54.7-10.KJV

"Heal me, O LORD, and I shall be healed; save me, and I shall be saved: for thou art my praise."
(Jeremiah 17:14 KJV)
https://bible.com/bible/1/jer.17.14.KJV20

"Having abolished in his flesh the enmity, even the law of commandments contained in ordinances; for to make in himself of twain one new man, so making peace; and that he might reconcile both unto God in one body by the cross, having slain the enmity thereby: and came and preached

peace to you which were afar off, and to them that were nigh. For through him we both have access by one Spirit unto the Father. Now therefore ye are no more strangers and foreigners, but fellow citizens with the saints, and of the household of God; and are built upon the foundation of the apostles and prophets, Jesus Christ himself being the chief corner stone;"
(Ephesians 2:15-20 KJV)
https://bible.com/bible/1/eph.2.15-20.KJV

"And I said, my strength and my hope is perished from the Lord: Remembering mine affliction and my misery, the wormwood and the gall. My soul hath them still in remembrance, and is humbled in me. This I recall to my mind, therefore have I hope. It is of the Lord's mercies that we are not consumed, because his compassions fail not. They are new every morning: great is thy faithfulness. The Lord is my portion, saith my soul; therefore will I hope in him. The Lord is good unto them that wait for him, to the soul that seeketh him."
(Lamentations 3:18-25 KJV)
https://bible.com/bible/1/lam.3.18-25.KJV

"Verily I say unto you, Whatsoever ye shall bind on earth shall be bound in heaven: and whatsoever ye shall loose on earth shall be loosed in heaven. Again I say unto you, That if two of you shall agree on earth as touching any thing that they shall ask, it shall be done for them of my Father which is in heaven. For where two or three are gathered together in my name, there am I in the midst of them."
(Matthew 18:18-20 KJV)

https://bible.com/bible/1/mat.18.18-20.KJV
"And Jesus answering saith unto them, Have faith in God. For verily I say unto you, That whosoever shall say unto this mountain, Be thou removed, and be thou cast into the sea; and shall not doubt in his heart, but shall believe that those things which he saith shall come to pass; he shall have whatsoever he saith. Therefore I say unto you, What things soever ye desire, when ye pray, believe that ye receive them, and ye shall have them. And when ye stand praying, forgive, if ye have ought against any: that your Father also which is in heaven may forgive you your trespasses. But if ye do not forgive, neither will your Father which is in heaven forgive your trespasses."
(Mark 11:22-26 KJV)
https://bible.com/bible/1/mrk.11.22-26.KJV

"But the fruit of the Spirit is love, joy, peace, longsuffering, gentleness, goodness, faith, Meekness, temperance: against such there is no law. And they that are Christ's have crucified the flesh with the affections and lusts. If we live in the Spirit, let us also walk in the Spirit. Let us not be desirous of vain glory, provoking one another, envying one another."
(Galatians 5:22-26 KJV)
https://bible.com/bible/1/gal.5.22-26.KJV

"Blessed be the God and Father of our Lord Jesus Christ, who hath blessed us with all spiritual blessings in heavenly places in Christ: According as he hath chosen us in him before the foundation of the world, that we should be holy and without blame before him in love: Having predestined us unto the adoption of children by Jesus Christ to himself, according to

the good pleasure of his will, to the praise of the glory of his grace, wherein he hath made us accepted in the beloved. In whom we have redemption through his blood, the forgiveness of sins, according to the riches of his grace; Wherein he hath abounded toward us in all wisdom and prudence; Having made known unto us the mystery of his will, according to his good pleasure which he hath purposed in himself: That in the dispensation of the fullness of times he might gather together in one all things in Christ, both which are in heaven, and which are on earth; even in him: In whom also we have obtained an inheritance, being predestined according to the purpose of him who worketh all things after the counsel of his own will: That we should be to the praise of his glory, who first trusted in Christ."
(Ephesians 1:3-12 KJV)
https://bible.com/bible/1/eph.1.3-12.KJV

"But God commandeth his love toward us, in that, while we were yet sinners, Christ died for us. Much more then, being now justified by his blood, we shall be saved from wrath through him. For if, when we were enemies, we were reconciled to God by the death of his Son, much more, being reconciled, we shall be saved by his life. And not only so, but we also joy in God through our Lord Jesus Christ, by whom we have now received the atonement."
(Romans 5:8-11 KJV)
https://bible.com/bible/1/rom.5.8-11.KJV

"For thou wilt light my candle: the Lord my God will enlighten my darkness. For by thee I have run through a troop; and by my God have I leaped over a wall. As for God, his way is

perfect: the word of the Lord is tried: he is a buckler to all those that trust in him. For who is God save the Lord? or who is a rock save our God? It is God that girdeth me with strength, and maketh my way perfect. He maketh my feet like hinds' feet, and setteth me upon my high places."
(Psalm 18:28-33 KJV)
https://bible.com/bible/1/psa.18.28-33.KJV

"Blessed is the man that walketh not in the counsel of the ungodly, nor standeth in the way of sinners, nor sitteth in the seat of the scornful. But his delight is in the law of the Lord; and in his law doth he meditate day and night. And he shall be like a tree planted by the rivers of water, that bringeth forth his fruit in his season; his leaf also shall not wither; and whatsoever he doeth shall prosper."
(Psalm 1:1-3 KJV)

"And the Lord said unto Satan, Hast thou considered my servant Job, that there is none like him in the earth, a perfect and an upright man, one that feareth God, and escheweth evil? and still he holdeth fast his integrity, although thou movedst me against him, to destroy him without cause."
(Job 2:3 KJV)
https://bible.com/bible/1/job.2.3.KJV

"Deliver me, I pray thee, from the hand of my brother, from the hand of Esau: for I fear him, lest he will come and smite me, and the mother with the children. And thou saidst, I will surely do thee good, and make thy seed as the sand of the sea, which cannot be numbered for multitude."
(Genesis 32:11-12 KJV)

https://bible.com/bible/1/gen.32.11-12.KJV
https://bible.com/bible/1/psa.1.1-3.KJV

"There shall not any man be able to stand before thee all the days of thy life: as I was with Moses, so I will be with thee: I will not fail thee, nor forsake thee. Be strong and of a good courage: for unto this people shalt thou divide for an inheritance the land, which I sware unto their fathers to give them. Only be thou strong and very courageous, that thou mayest observe to do according to all the law, which Moses my servant commanded thee: turn not from it to the right hand or to the left, that thou mayest prosper whithersoever thou goest. This book of the law shall not depart out of thy mouth; but thou shalt meditate therein day and night, that thou mayest observe to do according to all that is written therein: for then thou shalt make thy way prosperous, and then thou shalt have good success. Have not I commanded thee? Be strong and of a good courage; be not afraid, neither be thou dismayed: for the Lord thy God is with thee whithersoever thou goest."
(Joshua 1:5-9 KJV)
https://bible.com/bible/1/jos.1.5-9.KJV

"For therein is the righteousness of God revealed from faith to faith: as it is written, The just shall live by faith."
(Romans 1:17 KJV)
https://bible.com/bible/1/rom.1.17.KJV

"The law of the LORD is perfect, converting the soul: The testimony of the LORD is sure, making wise the simple. The statutes of the LORD are right, rejoicing the heart: The

commandment of the LORD is pure, enlightening the eyes. The fear of the LORD is clean, enduring for ever: The judgments of the LORD are true and righteous altogether. More to be desired are they than gold, yea, than much fine gold: Sweeter also than honey and the honeycomb. Moreover by them is thy servant warned: And in keeping of them there is great reward."
(Psalm 19:7-11 KJV)
https://bible.com/bible/1/psa.19.7-11.KJV

"And let the beauty of the LORD our God be upon us: And establish thou the work of our hands upon us; Yea, the work of our hands establish thou it."
(Psalm 90:17 KJV)
https://bible.com/bible/1/psa.90.17.KJV

"And I, if I be lifted up from the earth, will draw all men unto me. This he said, signifying what death he should die. The people answered him, We have heard out of the law that Christ abideth for ever: and how sayest thou, The Son of man must be lifted up? who is this Son of man? Then Jesus said unto them, Yet a little while is the light with you. Walk while ye have the light, lest darkness come upon you: for he that walketh in darkness knoweth not whither he goeth. While ye have light, believe in the light, that ye may be the children of light. These things spake Jesus, and departed, and did hide himself from them. But though he had done so many miracles before them, yet they believed not on him.
"(John 12:32-37 KJV)

Inspiring Poetry Corner

This is the first poem I remember recording in November 2013. I wrote it in my notebook while sitting next to the aeroplane window on my way to Jamaica for my second holiday since moving to the UK in November 1997, the year Princess Diana died. My first trip back to Jamaica was in 2007, and that was after being in England for a whole 10 years.

We were flying above the clouds and I just felt the awesome power of God's creative mind! My heart filled up with praise to the One who thought of and brought into being something so beautifully spectacular. I felt Almost close enough to reach out and touch these fluffy white clouds with the sun's rays glinting off them. The words just filled up my mind so that I wanted to record them:

My Walk with Christ

BEAUTY IN POWER

Look! Have you noticed
The beauty of the skies?
The clouds, Oh how I would
Love to touch them, fly
Into them, dance and play
Around them

I looked as far as my eyes could see
Way above the clouds.
They make funny patterns
On the sky ....but wait!
Now they are not higher than I.

God's beautiful creation
Salutes His majesty
And awesome power
He walks on the curves
Of the wind, and holds
A thunder bolt in His hand.

The same gentle hand
Lifts me up in love and
Let's me know that He is near.

My Walk with Christ

BEING ME, BEING YOU

I could never be you!
I cannot do what you do, like you?
I am way too busy working out the best way to be me.

I love doing what I do, the way that I can do :)
I love the way my eyes shine and how my dimples deepen when I smile.

When I walk, there is purpose in my stride...
What do you like most about you?
Enjoy you! Express you!
Let the world see the blessing that is you!
I like you just as you are!

I like how you brighten the room when you appear.
How you do everything with such flair...
Don't dim your light for anyone.

Don't you dare give up on your dream!
Like me, you are here to make a difference.
Like me your life is filled with flavour!

Let us add Godly taste to everyone we meet.
Transforming conversations for good...

My Walk with Christ

WHAT IS FAITH

FAITH is believing, when everyone else is doubting!
FAITH is staying, when everyone else is leaving!
FAITH is knowing that my inadequacy or failure won't stop God's perfect plan from being fulfilled in me.
FAITH is continuing to stand when there's no obvious reasons why you should.
FAITH is believing that the sun will come out again even after the most terrific storm.
FAITH is knowing that if I keep moving in the right direction, I will reach my destination.
FAITH is staying focused, in the midst of chaos.
FAITH is setting goals and making definite plans that I want to achieve.
FAITH is being willing to trust in the wisdom of godly counsel
FAITH is trusting that God who has created us, can save us, keep us in this life and the next.
FAITH IS WHAT KEEPS HOPE ALIVE!!!

My Walk with Christ

Sometimes I Feel Like a Fraud

If I think about doing something that is really important and the feeling of panic and self-doubt comes up in me, I will switch to something else that reduces that feeling of fear, panic or inadequacy.

I don't consistently write my goals or to-do lists because I feel this shows up my failure. So I continue to let myself fail with no accountability.

How do I start to change my future expectations?
How do I affirm my self-worth?
How do I live my best life?
How do I gain strength to accomplish and achieve God's great purpose for me?

My Walk with Christ

CELEBRATE

Start to celebrate ME
Write down my achievements each day and celebrate. Give God thanks that He helped me accomplish something extraordinary that I didn't know I could do. Celebrate!
Write down my skills and talents, things that I do well – and celebrate!

Celebrating the positives about me
builds resilience and courage to change my outlook, my reality, my truth.
CELEBRATE!

The Lord did not make a mistake when He created me! He had
a specific plan in His mind. He knew that I could accomplish. He knew that I could excel!
He knew that I would sometimes stumble...
He knew that I would sometimes fail..
He never at any time doubted that I would accomplish His will.

Lord thank you for your grace and favour, your patient endurance and still; you faithfully tell me each morning, "REMAIN IN MY PRESENCE, STAY IN MY WILL,"
Forever and ever Lord Jesus I'll stay in your presence and will. I'll love and honour your name Lord. I'll follow wherever you lead.

My Walk with Christ

The light of your presence LORD Jesus, makes clear the path where I tread..

Whenever I lose focus dear Father,
whenever my strength seems to fail,
Whenever I forget who I am Lord.
Please put a song in my heart and remind me how much I have to be thankful for and to:
CELEBRATE 🙏 🙏

PURPOSE CANNOT DIE

When the persons God entrusted you (His precious seed, unpolished diamond, gold nugget) to parent, shepherd, partner or mentor, and any one of them decide to bury you, it's either because of fear or laziness or lack of vision. You've got to allow your seed to travel deep into the soil and find moisture. Follow the call of your Creator; the urge to live. Follow the direction of great strong trees with deep roots. Why? Because one day, you are going to need to burst through that (mighty soil as a tiny seedling! You're going to have to keep growing roots down to keep your buds growing up and live!

You're going to have to be patient and determined to keep growing, because your purpose is waiting for you.

Other trees around you are at different stages of their development. You might be the smallest, most underdeveloped looking one in your forest. The other, bigger trees might make fun of your size, or shape or your seemingly slow development but they don't know how far down you're coming from, or how strong are your roots.

Your age does not determine your usefulness or value. Your stage of development, your readiness and your ability to competently complete your assignment; will determine your success.

My Walk with Christ

Within every seed there is a specific purpose. Within every person's DNA is a unique plan, placed there by God's own thought. In love and with grace He gifted us to Himself!

Purpose is waiting

Choosing Christ is the only CHOICE

Just like Jesus Christ, our lives are constantly under attack from our enemy (Satan). The enemy doesn't just give up after one failed attempt.
From the time of our birth right up until we leave this earth, we will face fierce opposition from our foe.

Satan knows our worth, our potential, our abilities. He is privy to our God given purpose. He has been reading up on us, done his research and knows how much of a threat we are to his Kingdom! So he strategises, he plans very carefully about how to distract, derail, disappoint and delay us from fulfilling God's plan and purpose for our lives., Because we live in limited time and space, we tend to react naturally using our emotions. For example: FEAR of LOSS. We fear losing our family, friends, culture, identity, control etc. The enemy uses fear to try and control us to an emotional response. Our Father God knows how we are likely to react because He made us! He has more importantly provided us with the means to overcome the temptations by way of His Spirit. The Apostle Paul reminds us that *"The weapons of our warfare are not carnal (emotional, natural), but mighty throughGod."* (2Cor.10:4).

The Lord Jesus Christ our Saviour, our example, was also tempted just like us, but He never lost His way.

(Heb. 4:15). He was fully human just like us, living to fulfil His purpose, in limited time and space, to be able to deliver us from the power of our enemy Satan, who has spiritual power, being the prince of the power of the air, who controls people through their emotions (natural reactions), which takes them further away from their purpose to connect with their creator and fulfil their God ordained purpose.

Jesus Christ lived as one of us, among us and for us; unto God. He connected with the Father always. He did what the Father commanded Him to do. He did not promote His human greatness but the perfection of the Father. (Luke 18:19; Psalm 100:5). He would seek out those who were in need to bless, heal and feed them! He always welcomed and sought to serve, affirm and comfort the weak and downtrodden. He admonished, corrected fellowship with the rich and powerful, even though He knew that they were against Him..

Christ Jesus fulfilled His purpose! He came to seek and to save those who are and were lost, to bind up the broken hearted and set the oppressed free, to deliver us from the power of sin and death, to restore us back to right standing with God.

Now that we are saved, free, restored, Spirit filled, we are responsible to make the choices that Jesus Christ our redeemer example, made. To first of all be always connected with our Father through His Spirit in prayer and the Word. Be humble and serve others as He did. Promote the goodness and

greatness of God and not ourselves. Seek to save those who are lost. Be willing to die for the sake of Christ, so we can live in victory inspite of the constant attacks from our enemy.
(Mathew 10:37)

To have victory in battle, a soldier must be prepared! This takes time, effort and a great deal of self-sacrifice. Once the decision has been made, intense training must begin. This soldier has to leave family, friends, culture even ownership of self behind. From here on in this person is owned by the military. They will be trained to first of all listen to and obey the commands of their superior officers; they will be issued with uniforms that have to be kept and worn exactly according to the rules. They have to learn to work as part of a team (their lives depend on this). They have to learn the different methods of combat both offensive and defensive. They have to learn the international rules of war and how to survive if captured by the enemy. (Rom.12:2; 8:29)

By the time this soldier has completed their training, they will have become, aware of where their allegiance lays. They'll be stronger physically, mentally, even emotionally, focused and sure of their mission . Even more importantly they will know how to fulfil their purpose! With continued practice in obedience, learning, team building and working, this soldier will become better, wiser, stronger and possibly a great leader. To fulfil our

God ordained purpose, we must be willing to make the tough choice. As the Lord admonished His disciples to deny themselves, take up their cross and follow Him. He also reassured them that by giving up everything to follow Him they were making room to receive blessings and provisions that were beyond their greatest dreams. And so it is for us! Let us step out in faith, believing what we cannot see, trusting for what we hope for. Knowing that God is faithful. He will not go back on His Word. We are conquerors through Him that loved us and gave up His glory just to bring us back to Himself.
Put on the whole armour of God so as to be able to stand against the wiles of the devil.
In the power of God we stand.

What is Love?

Love is patient
Love is kind
Love bears all things
Hope in all things
Believe and expect the best from all things
Love is not big headed or self-seeking,
Is not easily angered
Love is not vengeful or spiteful in any way,
Does not seek to highlight the negative side of others but instead, try to see the positives in every situation.
Love transcends the limits of human understanding and reveals the nature of God.
Love does not promote evil, only the truth.
Love lift up and strengthen the weak
Gives bread to the hungry and
Hides the shame of the naked.
Love is long-suffering; believing for a good outcome.
Love is the greatest gift of God to man.
Love is man's best response to God and each other.

My Walk with Christ

THE ECHOES OF STRENGTH

I sat on the edge of my bed and I heard the voices of our ancestors and saw them shackled together in the darkness. Scared, frightened, yet strong and fierce! Determined to live! They could only communicate through deep groanings: expressing their pain and confusion and desire to hope! Hope that somehow there will come a time when this will end and they will be free. Today this groaning is still echoing through the ages. The warrior spirit in us refuses to die or be defeated. Christ Jesus came and gave us deliverance that is far more than physical or national. It's generational and eternal. Today we declare freedom!!! While praying for all who are still bound. For all who are oppressed and in particular for those who are so blind that they still think they have the power to enslave and oppress.
Heavenly Father Saviour Lord, please help!

BELIEVE IT IS DONE

Now the Lord is that Spirit: and where the Spirit of the Lord is, there is liberty. But we all, with open face beholding as in a glass the glory of the Lord, are changed into the same image from glory to glory, even as by the Spirit of the Lord.
(2 Corinthians 3:17-18 KJV)
https://bible.com/bible/1/2co.3.17-18.KJV

For the weapons of our warfare are not of the flesh! By the flesh, or through the flesh!

For though we walk in the flesh, we do not war after the flesh: (For the weapons of our warfare are not carnal, but mighty through God to the pulling down of strong holds;) Casting down imaginations, and every high thing that exalteth itself against the knowledge of God, and bringing into captivity every thought to the obedience of Christ;
(2 Corinthians 10:3-5 KJV)
https://bible.com/bible/1/2co.10.3-5.KJV

Never allow what other people say or do to influence the level of your success or your beliefs in the possibilities that you dream of, and hope for. It is Christ who gives good dreams and hopes. It is His Spirit that stirs us to action so that we can fulfil our destiny as He our creator envisioned for us.

My Walk with Christ

He transferred His vision plans into us even before we were born. So we feel driven and excited about reaching, making, climbing, producing developing..... Then something happens...
Someone who we look to, or trust, does or says something...
They have their own idea of who you should be and are willing to do everything possible to prevent you being God's idea of who you are.
DON'T LET THEM.....
Continue to believe and speak over yourself; encourage yourself in the Lord.
Remember, the Lord said; "Before one jot or tittle of my Word pass, Heaven and Earth shall pass."
That also means what He has promised to you and me.
The Lord has paid the price for our freedom so why, like the children of Israel in the wilderness, are we still holding on to the state of bondage?
Being crippled in our minds and refusing to see by faith, the 'promised land'. The fulfilment of that dream?
If you have faith like a mustard seed, you can speak to that mountain.....
Anything is possible to those who believe....
With man it is impossible but with God all things are possible.
Abraham believed God. He left his country, his family, his safe place and went where God sent him. He also did what God told him to do, even to the giving up of his only son. So God honoured

My Walk with Christ

Abraham's faith and granted him wealth, favour, success, influence and most importantly the promise of blessings to all his generations and even to all people in ages to come. That we who practice uncommon faith in God, would also inherit the promise.

God will also honour our faith in Him by giving us what we ask for. Exceeding abundantly more than we can possibly envision; by His power that is at work in us; through Jesus Christ, for the glory of His Name. Every plan that God has for us is possible. His vision, dream, desire for our lives will produce the best outcome. Legacies that dreams are made of will manifest for us, our families and our communities...

So in spite of the fiery furnace or the lion's den or the wilderness experiences; dream large! Dream loud! Dream in brilliant colours! Commit every work to Christ and seek His perfect will.. The Spirit Word of God still speaks through the ages. "It's not by might nor by power, but by my Spirit; saith the Lord". Zech 4:6

My Walk with Christ

Minister Judy's Poems

My Walk with Christ

GOD WATCH OVER YOU

God see beautiful pictures of my adventurous life,
The dangers that I faced
Living in a fast pace,
Many would not survive,
Not without God's grace,
But I have a Refuge,
In THE ROCK I will hide.

God knows about,
The traps and snares set
To destroy, my precious life,
I live in the wilds,
The creatures of prey.
And the changing seasons,
Threatens my existence,
But my life is hid with Christ in God.

God is in control,
He knows about the strong holds,
It is amazing, when my life seems
Like It's going wrong,
It turns out right
Let's say it's a set up
The step of a good man,
Is ordered by the Lord.

Jesus loved and cares,
About my victorious life,
Let the wind blow,

My Walk with Christ

Let the storm cloud rise,
Let the thunder roll,
Let the lightening flash
In all these things, I am confident,
God is working it out for my good.

My Walk with Christ

LOVE WORTH FINDING

I had a sweet dream
I'm sure it's love I had seen,
Deep in my being,
Love's tender affection I had felt,
My heart pounded, my spirit enraptured,
Ascends into love's pure realm,
No strength to resist, compelled,
To submit I yield,
There in love's trance, I imagined,
If it's real.

Love is like fire,
I had felt the heat of its desire,
It burns passionately sweet,
I never wanted to retreat,
Always needs a repeat,
This made me laugh,
With pleasure from my heart,
One experience, with love eternal treat,
Made me realised, no other can compete.

My Walk with Christ

GOD SEES YOU

Jesus does not see the crowd,
He sees you,
In the tumult of your life,
He hears your faintest cry,
Jesus is the good shepherd,
His sheep He will identify.

Jesus knows your deepest needs,
You don't even have to tell,
His loving eyes,
And bright countenance,
Penetrates deep into your soul,
Reveal the secret your mind control.

Jesus is the source and power
To Him you can come boldly,
Find grace and strength,
Like night turns to day,
Your inner beauty, unfolds,
All darkness, deadness
Surrendered their hold.

My Walk with Christ

CRAZY LOVE

Love is crazy and out of control,
Blinded by passionate desires,
Love knows no barrier,
What shall separate you from God
There is no fear in perfect love,
Love search for you like a dove,
Sent from heaven above.

Love never rested but relentlessly,
Seeks, to fulfil its dreams,
With love there is no respect of persons,
Are you bound and in prison?
Love will come in the midnight hour,
By His power,
Break the chains and set you free.

Love is High and Supreme
Yet condescend to our lowly estate,
Are you lowly for love?
His strong arms will lift you up,
Whoever you are,
Where ever you are,
Love is available to you all.

My Walk with Christ

CHURCH LIFE

Church is like my home,
In it I roam,
I am never alone,
Sometimes when in a meeting,
We should give the greetings
But we end up eating,
Some of us start sleeping,

Chop, chop wake up,
It's time to drink the cup,
Each one received a sup,
In this there can be no hiccup,
The pastor said let us pray,
This is not the time to play,
Your blessings will not be delay.

THE FIVE SENSES OF LOVE

Flames leaped up, out of my heart,
As the fire of love burns, deep within,
The desire of love always longed,
To touch,
To hold,
To feel
It's ecstasy and passion,

I wish for an encounter
The joining of two souls,
That delightfully mingles,
The five senses,
Seeing,
Hearing,
Feeling,
Smelling,
Tasting you, O LORD.

My Walk with Christ

TAKE COURAGE AND TRY

Don't think I am shy,
When I start to cry,
I feel so under-minded,
Never wanted to try,

The subject was hard,
That I will not deny,
By my teacher standard,
I have to strive high,

With great courage,
I took on the task,
Never want to come last,
Everyone expects me to pass.

My Walk with Christ

FIGHT

Ray a drop of golden sun light,
And music to drive away your plight,
Although the way is dark,
By the shadows of the night,
Combine music with light,
And you will find strength to fight.

MY HEART YIELDS

God's love is so real

I love the way He make me feel,

When He hold me close in His arms,

My heart yield to His tender embrace,

And all my fears He erase.

Never felt such sweet love

This only comes from the father about.

He dries all my tears,

I know that He cares,

No more sighing, no more crying,

With my heart filled with joy

Praise God He's my all in all.

My Walk with Christ

LET ME SING

I saw angels in the heavenly choir,

They open their wings as they sing

Praises to the king,

Oh the joy that I felt, within my soul enraptured,

Oh let me sing

Praises to the king of kings.

Oh Let me sing

Let me sing of His grace

Let me sing of the wonders of God's love. Repeat

One day I'll join the heavenly choir,

With saints appearing in glory,

We'll sing glad songs

and tell our story,

How we overcome

Oh let me sing

Praises to the king of kings.

My Walk with Christ

BRAND NEW START

I had been so afraid on the altar I laid,

My heart's been hurting from the pain of the past,

So I needed a brand new start.

Brand new start, brand new start,

Jesus came and He gave me a brand new .

Darkness filled my life, my way I could not see,

He holds my hand, and guides me with His eyes,

Now I can feel the sun shining,

I know it's a brighter day,

So I needed a brand new start.

My Walk with Christ

VICTORY IN JESUS NAME

I was so lost in sin

Fighting a battle by myself

I could not win,

The conflict was sore,

I could not take anymore,

But when it seems that all hope is lost,

My help came when I called on Jesus name.

For I remember 'twas for me

He died on Calvary

Now I'm rejoicing, my battles

are won,

The enemy's been defeated, and my soul been set free

      Thank God, Jesus gives me victory.

My Walk with Christ

Inspiring Quotes

Paster Neruka White

A difficult crisis can be more readily endured if we retain the conviction that our existence holds a purpose;
A cause to pursue, a person to love,
A goal to achieve.

John C Maxwell

You have not lived today until you have done something for someone who can never repay you.

John Bunyan

When one door closes
another opens.
But we often look so
long and so regretfully
upon the closed door
That we do not see the
one
Which has opened for
us.

Alexander Graham Bell

I have learned that success is to be measured not so much by the position That one has reached in life as by the obstacles which one has overcome while trying to succeed.

Booker T Washington

Don't let yourself WORRY when you're doing your best.
HURRY when success depends on accuracy.
THINK evil of anyone until you have the facts
BELIEVE a thing is Impossible without trying it.

Pastor Neruka White

My Walk with Christ

Inspiring Quotes

Judy Creighton

The weight of sin is depressing, cast it on Jesus.

Humility precedes honour.

It is a terrible sin not to believe God.

When you are in love the shadows are beautiful

*Do not let the
volcano of life
burn out your oil.*

God will make you humble, by breaking you in the right places.

In my heart I make room for pleasure.

You will be rewarded if you finish your race.

You cannot find peace until you find all the pieces.

Unbelief is an addiction which numbs the soul.

The taste of defeat makes winning more desirable.

LETTER TO MY YOUNGER SELF

Dear, Little Neruka (Ner)

Precious first daughter of Joseph and Bernice. You are treasured by God who has anointed and appointed you for great things. Remember what Granny Addy said about dedicating you to the service of the Lord on the day you were born? How Granny has spent a major part of her mid to senior years to love, help, guide, teach and protect you? That is the love and faithfulness of God honouring Granny's prayer.

Be brave little girl. Good manners will take you through the world, Granny's said. Where you are at any given time, you are not alone, not abandoned, not rejected. But in training. The light in your eyes and brightness of your smile, the easy way you fit in makes you stand out from the crowd.

Even though you're not growing up with your parents and siblings, the times that you spend with them will be memorable, both the negative and positive experiences are meant to help shape who you will become. You are always loved, always valued.

Even in your tender years when what you have seems so small and not enough, you're learning life's important lessons of gratitude and making the most of what you have. Learning is such a pleasure for you, and teaching too.

Don't worry too much about rejection even though this really hurts. Some people, places and things are really better from a distance. Take every opportunity to learn the lessons life is teaching you. Be observant, less trusting and more confident in the power, strength and courage God has given you. Do not be afraid of the predators, naysayers or those who can't see your value. The most precious stones are hidden in the dark, deep undercover of rocks and soil. Mining is a rough job and crafting is done by the one with the vision and creative power to turn the rough stone into beautiful jewellery, fit for the King's crown.

Celebrate the small achievements and keep believing in your dreams because the purpose for which you were created, will surely be fulfilled.

Children and adults who you so gently give your time and talents to, form your social network and extended family; valuable lessons will be learned. Here you will discover that family is not only those related by blood. The love and acceptance you receive here can make the difference between hope and despair. Treasure the good gifts you are given. Learn the hard lessons not a few.

My Walk with Christ

Forgive all those who hurt you; there's only so far they can go. God Himself built a strong hedge all around you, to keep your life from destruction and make you a message of love. So spread out your wings little girl, keep soaring with the eagles because that is where you belong.

Your more experienced self,

Love,

Pastor Neruka

My Walk with Christ

Dear Little Judy,

I know you. You are young and beautiful. You are intelligent and gifted.
I know that you struggled to believe in yourself. Fear is your biggest enemy.

Some of your childhood experiences have played a big part in influencing how you think about yourself.

I know about the time when you won two prizes. You were seven years old, a grade one student. You achieved these prizes for attendance and for your grades. You came first in your class.

Your prizes were taken away from you by fellow students. They were very jealous of your success. I remember you holding two large cakes in your hands. The evil children took and smashed your cakes and scattered them on the ground.

I know how you felt because you wanted to share your success with your family, especially with your grandmother who was your guardian. That experience had traumatised you and that negative energy has caused you to think less of yourself.

You thought that you were not worthy of success. You developed low self-esteem. I know that you had other similar experiences that have reinforced those negative emotions. But you are strong. Take

My Walk with Christ

courage. I want you to know that the power is within you to succeed.

Never give up. Keep on striving. You can achieve all your dreams. The sky is the limit. Keep on moving. If you can't run, walk. If you can't walk, crawl, but whatever you do, keep on growing. Your future is bright.

To you with all my love
From your future self.

Judy Creighton

My Walk with Christ

Favourite Gospel Songs

Selected Neruka White

GOD WILL MAKE A WAY
(Don Moen)
God will make a way, where there seems to be no way.
He works in ways you cannot see.
He will make a way for me..

LET HIM HAVE HIS WAY WITH THEE
(Cyrus S Nusbaum)
Would you live for Jesus and be always
pure and good? Would you walk with Him within
the narrow road? Would you have Him share your
burden carry all your load?
Let Him have His way with thee.

HE'LL DO IT AGAIN
(Shirley Caeser)
You may feel down and think that God has
somehow forgotten
That you are faced with circumstances
You cannot get through

LORD PLANT MY FEET
(Charles H Gabriel)
I'm pressing on the upward way
New heights I'm gaining every day

My Walk with Christ

Still praying as I onward bound
Lord plant my feet on higher ground.

HOME OF THE SOUL
(Ellen H Gates)
If for the prize we have striven
After our labours are o'er
Rest to our souls will be given
On the eternal shore.

NOTHING BETWEEN
(F A Clark)
Nothing between myself and my Saviour
Nought of this world delusion dream
I have renounce all sinful pleasure
Jesus is mine, there's nothing between.

HE KNOWS MY NAME
(Tasha Cobs Leonard)
Oh how He walks with me
Ye how He talks with me
And oh how He tells me
That I am His own

I DON'T NEED MY NAME IN LIGHTS
(Francesca Battiistelli)
I don't need my name in lights
I'm famous in my Father's eyes
Make no mistake, He knows my name
I'm not living for applause...

THE BLOOD
(Andrè Crouch)
The blood that Jesus shed for me
Way back on Calvary, the blood
That gives me strength from day to day
It will never lose its power.

THROUGH IT ALL
(Andrè Crouch)
Through it all, through it all
I've learned to trust in Jesus
I've learned to trust in God
Through it all through it all
I've learned to depend upon His Word.

Epilogue

God knows the challenges that we may face on our life's journey and wants us to know that He cares. Through every challenge we gain experiences, therefore we've all got a story.

Your story can inspire a generation and give hope to many people. My life experience taught me that I should always believe that God is able to make a way where there seems to be no way. Therefore I should never lose sight of hope.

People are always seeking for answers to their problems. The answers that you seek are only a prayer away. God is our heavenly father. He hears and He answers prayer.

THE IMPORTANCE OF PRAYER

And it came to pass, that, as he was praying in a certain place, when he ceased, one of his disciples said unto him, Lord, teach us to pray, as John also taught his disciples. And he said unto them, When ye pray, say, Our Father which art in heaven, Hallowed be thy name. Thy kingdom come. Thy will be done, as in heaven, so in earth. And forgive us our sin; for we also forgive every one that is indebted to us. And lead us not into temptation; but deliver us from evil.

(Luke 11:1-2, 4 KJV)

Q. What is prayer?

A. Prayer is having a conversation with God. There are different types of prayer, e.g. making requests or supplications for ourselves or others, prayers of thanks giving (worship), praying in tongues, prayers of repentance and intercessory prayers, which are made on behalf of another person.

Q. How must we pray?

A. By following the guidelines given by Jesus in Mathew 6 and Luke 11. We must approach God with humbleness, reverence and thankfulness (worship). We must speak to Him as our Father and listen for His answers and we must spend time being quiet in His presence. Read the Bible and reflect on what we have read; We might find the answers to our questions or requests there.

Q. Why must we pray?

A. Because praying is much more than asking for stuff; rather, we should have a conversation with the Lord. It's most important for us to pray always, as prayer keeps us connected to our spiritual and natural source of life. Prayer gives us confidence to know that we can talk to God about everything and He has the right answers, solutions and provisions for all our needs. Prayer provides a safe space where we can be open and honest, confess our failures, fears, misconceptions and receive forgiveness, correction, encouragement and strength.

Q. When should we pray?

A. First of all, Jesus says we must be ready to pray all the time. Praying at specific times are good, as this helps us to have a routine; such as first thing in the morning and last thing at night. Praying at Church is also very important, whether alone or together with others. We should pray for ourselves, our families, neighbours, leaders, friends, enemies, government, teachers, bus drivers, the sick, homeless, the bad people. We should talk to God all the time.

Stay connected with Him, be conscious that He is always with us. Not to make us afraid but to help us be free from bondage of sin that separates us from Him. To give us confidence and courage to love what is right and good so that we will be the leaders wherever we are, living as ambassadors of the Kingdom of Heaven. Let us start each day with a prayer of thanksgiving to The Lord, acknowledging that He is the giver and sustainer of our most valuable gift, life!Our Father in Heaven, thank you for my life and for all of us who are here today. May we live today in a way that brings blessings to others and honour to your Name. Amen

My Walk with Christ

About the Authors

Pastor Neruka White

My Name is Neruka White. I was born in a little house on Old Harbour Road, Spanish Town, Jamaica, a wonderful 62 years ago.

I spent most of my growing up years with my paternal grandmother; she was always a very great force who stood between me and terrible dangers on more occasions than I can count. I learnt some of my best life skills from my grandma. She taught me the importance of having a close relationship with the Lord Jesus Christ. Praying and reciting verses from the scriptures was as important as going to school. My grandma sang all the time and encouraged me to learn many hymns and choruses that we sang at church.

One of the skills granny taught me through her own life was to care for those who are in need, to give and share what I have with someone who might never be able to do something for me or even show gratitude.

I learned the value of having my own family and loving each person because of who they are and not what they have or are able to give.

Granny loved me with such strong dedication and honesty. She never made pretence about life's challenges. She talked with me about almost everything. I knew when we had much and when we had nothing. That helped me to feel free and learn to be content in any situation. I did not have unrealistic expectations. In fact, in spending time with my birth mother, I learned entrepreneurial skills, which encouraged independence and a determination to work and learn so that I wouldn't need to depend on anyone.

I love to teach. I think teaching is one of my superpowers, along with caring for people. Whatever I receive, whether it's learning something new, or physical things and resources, I automatically look for someone to give to and share them with.

In 2009, as inspired by the Lord, I started Neruka's Soul Food Soup Kitchen. The aim was to provide a free meal to anyone who was in need. What a journey it has been these past thirteen years!

Many changes have happened as my team and I strived to remain true to the vision plan which is: to minister to the people in the church community through the provision of food.

Neruka's Soul Food Soup Kitchen is now a registered charity that continues to provide food and other resources by partnering with different organisations in the city of Leeds.

More information can be found on the website:
www.nerukassoulfood.co.uk

After the heavenly transition of our pastor, Bishop Lionel C Currie, I was told that the honour and responsibility of leading and caring for the church in Leeds was now given to me and my husband, Elder Paul White.

We moved to Leeds from London in December 1999 and became part of this assembly immediately and have served the Lord where, how and when He has tasked us.

I've served in different organisations in the city of Leeds. I volunteered for over ten years with the council led Leeds Tenants Federation, sitting on various panels, representing the rights and interests of LCC tenants; and also as a tenant representative on the local Housing Advisory Panel (HAP).

I was assistant secretary, then vice chair for the now defunct West Yorkshire African Caribbean Council of churches. I chaired our local churches Together group between 2000 and 2002, and again from 2019 to 2021. Founding members and part of the planning committee of the Leeds Foodaid Network that provides support and information for and about the wide range of food providers in Leeds who fight hunger and marginalisation of God's people.

I also started an online group to support women in ministry across the world in 2019. In 2022 we launched our first project in Jamaica. The Women of Valour Extraordinary Scholarship Program for Children in Jamaica. This ministry has worked with two Apostolic churches in St Catherine, Jamaica and supported a number of children in learning about bible characters they had never heard of before. Nine children in total have received financial support towards school supplies. Praise God. Our vision is to work with local churches across the fourteen parishes of Jamaica in an effort to introduce children to the good news of salvation through Jesus Christ, with the Word and practical help.

My Walk with Christ

Neruka's Soul Food Soup Kitchen
Registered charity, number: 1164484
Telephone: 07400 901282

1. **Useful Links:** www.nerukassoulfood.co.uk
2. www.ucb.co.uk/wordfortoday

https://podcasters.spotify.com/pod/show/neruka-white

My Walk with Christ

Minister Judy Creighton

My name is Judy Creighton. I am a minister of the Gospel of Jesus Christ and have been in the ministry since I was twenty years old. I have served in Jamaica and in the United Kingdom.

I was born in Jamaica and came to England in 1997. I am an entrepreneur and the founder of the Try It Caribbean Take Away based in Stafford, Staffordshire.

As a prayer minister, I have dedicated my life to fasting and prayer and have seen many of my prayer requests came to pass, including this book, My Walk With Christ.

www.kingdomtruthbibleschool.org

Reflections Study Notes

My Walk with Christ

My Walk with Christ

My Walk with Christ

My Walk with Christ

My Walk with Christ

My Walk with Christ

My Walk with Christ

My Walk with Christ

My Walk with Christ

My Walk with Christ

My Walk with Christ

Printed in Great Britain
by Amazon